JAPANESE MYTHOLOGY UNLEASHED

DISCOVER SHINTO DEITIES, YŌKAI, AND HISTORIC
HEROES ON A JOURNEY THROUGH ANCIENT JAPAN

ANTHONY POE

CONTENTS

Introduction   5

1. THE DAWN OF JAPANESE MYTHOLOGY   9
   The Birth of the World and the Gods   9
   Meeting the Shinto Deities   16
   Sacred Spaces in Mythology   25

2. LEGENDARY HEROES AND HEROINES   29
   The Emperor Jimmu   30
   Yamato Takeru—the Prince of Adventure   35
   Empress Jingu—the Conquering Heroine   44
   The Peach Boy and the Fisher Lad   49
   Echoes in the Samurai Ethos   58

3. YŌKAI —THE SUPERNATURAL CREATURES   63
   The Enigma of Yōkai   64
   Gallery of the Supernatural   65

4. MYTHS OF CREATION, DESTRUCTION, AND
   RENEWAL   87
   The Origins   88
   When Worlds End   89
   The Cycles of Seasons and Life   90

5. RITUALS, FESTIVALS, AND CULTURAL
   PRACTICES   101
   The Sacred Thread of Shinto Rituals   102
   The Calendar of Joy: Annual Festivals   111

6. INFLUENCE AND RELATIONSHIP TO OTHER
   CULTURES   119
   Neighboring Shores: Chinese and Korean Influences   119
   Similarities With Other Myths   123

Conclusion   129
References   131

INTRODUCTION

Imagine a scene: a woodland permeated by light, the sun's rays gently outlining the greenery with their golden hue. Amidst that natural greenness, a sudden shock of color: multiple T-shaped gates painted bright orange, inviting you to take a step into the unknown. Guided by curiosity, you walk below the gates; immediately, the sunlight feels different, filtered by the soaring orange. It feels like you are suddenly transported to a completely different world.

Finally, the path leads you to the destination: a wooden pagoda with sloping roofs, surrounded by cherry blossoms—a picture straight from a postcard. You have arrived at a Shinto shrine, a phenomenon native to the Japanese culture. But rather than simply taking nice pictures and posting them on your social media, you are curious. You want to know more about the religion and culture that built this place. You want to explore the beliefs that live there.

Now, imagine that you take the same mysterious path through the woods at dusk. The sun's rays can no longer find their way through the thicket, and it is getting dark quickly. At the first gate, you see a lonesome figure. As you step closer, you realize it is a woman. You want to ask her if she's also going to the shrine, but then you notice it: something isn't adding up. The woman's face is a picture of beauty, narrow with high cheekbones and thin eyebrows, but there is something... *cold* about her. Slightly wary, you take a step back. The woman turns away from you, and then you see it: a shadow of a fluffy tail—a fox's tail!

You blink in shock. Only minutes ago, you were roaming the streets of modern cities, looking at skyscrapers and wondering if any of the culture of ancient Japan managed to survive, and now? It seems you have encountered a *kitsune*—a fox spirit. Or, maybe it was only the shadows in the dusky forest that were playing tricks on you?

After all, you are in Japan. In every country, myths and legends serve as a backbone for a culture. They are the lens through which people of that culture see their past, present, and future. You probably experience it, too, even if you don't realize it. This fact is evident in Japan. Many of the ancient beliefs are not forgotten. The strange spirits still live there. This book will help you explore and understand them.

If you are even marginally interested in Japanese culture and history beyond the picturesque Shinto shrines, you probably associate it with three things: anime, manga, and the samurai tradition. Of course, this is an overly simplistic image; there is *way* more to Japan than that. Still, when we foreigners and newcomers to Japan perceive modern and slightly more ancient Japanese culture, it is mainly through these lenses. But chances are, if you choose to read my book, you want to know more.

s, Japan is a country of unique stories and characteristic styles, every fascination with a new manga or anime series brings questions about the possible inspiration behind the stories. Have you ever watched *Spirited Away* (2001) or read *Naruto* (1999–2014) and wondered where the spirits depicted there come from? Or, maybe you found yourself fascinated with the samurai culture and wanted to know more about their history and beliefs that guided their behavior—and perhaps even find something that could inspire you on your life journey.

What are the equivalents of No-Face from *Spirited Away* and Kurama from *Naruto* in Japanese myth and folklore? Why do the spirits and divine entities from Japan seem just so *different* from those of the Western world? Why are the human heroes so honorable and unique?

This book will answer your questions. We will take a deep dive—from the earliest sources and ancient tales to the modern day. We will look at how the Japanese tradition was formed and influenced by Shintoism. We will review the narratives about the creation of the world, and we will meet the iconic gods, goddesses, and heroes who form the core of the Japanese myth. We will be introduced to the *yōkai*, or the uniquely Japanese spirits. We will take part in rituals and festivals and take a closer look at many cultural practices that permeate the life of the Japanese people to this day. Finally, we will trace the influence of the ancient Japanese tradition both through space and time. We'll see how it played a role in the traditions of other countries and how it survived for hundreds of years, staying alive in the modern day and age.

Our journey won't be simply a catalog of gods, spirits, and heroes. As you probably realized from the scene I painted at the beginning of this introduction, the characters from the Japanese myth will be more than just contained in a glossary or an encyclopedia. They permeate time and space and are highly present in Japanese culture even to this day. Each story you will read will show you how this happened—how the ancient yōkai found their way to modern cities and how the spirits still roam the streets and live in the collective subconscious of the people.

I hope this journey will acquaint you not only with fascinating stories and characters but also with the people who created them —that you will better understand the people of Japan and their culture. You will see their hopes and fears with an open mind, recognizing both the uniqueness and the universal value of their experience. And if you happen to find yourself at an actual Shinto shrine, you will approach it with a more profound sense of openness.

So, let's step on the path and prepare for all that awaits you at the destination...

1

THE DAWN OF JAPANESE MYTHOLOGY

I magine total chaos...

These words may fail to capture what I want to convey. The typical depiction of chaos in our cluttered world often equals disorder and scattered items. However, the chaos I want you to imagine differs from the mess found in unattended rooms or dusty attics. Picture instead a shapeless, disorderly substance surrounded by absolute darkness. Frankly, this might be a challenge to your imagination. Yet, in Japanese mythology, this chaos describes the state of the universe before its creation. Let us now delve into the abyss...

THE BIRTH OF THE WORLD AND THE GODS

The Japanese creation myth begins philosophically, as shown in two eighth-century chronicles, *Kojiki* and *Nihon Shoki*. Instead of swiftly explaining how deities came to be, these ancient texts consider the mysterious state of existence—chaos. A mass of particles wandering in different directions characterized this initial state as it seemed destined for permanent disorder.

Suddenly, a moment of change occurred. The particles of light gradually started ascending. These particles lit up the entire universe when they united, creating a massive shift in the cosmic story.

As the light particles floated upward, the other particles slowly found their place in the different corners of the universe, all according to their mass. Soon, the lightest elements formed clouds, and the first actual location emerged: the Plain of High Heaven, also known as the *Takamagahara*—the birthplace of the Japanese gods.

Shortly after, the ancient mists that shaped the Heavenly High Plain gave rise to the first *kami*, or gods. However, the first three gods—Ame-no-Minakanushi ("Deity of the August Centre of Heaven"), Takami-Musubi (the "High Producing Wondrous Deity" or "High Creator"), and Kami-Musubi ("Divine Producing Wondrous Deity")—played only a tiny role in Japanese myths. Almost immediately after they emerged, they hid themselves. Notably, these deities were genderless and had no companions or counterparts.

All the while, the chaotic particles were finding their own places in the universe. The heaviest of them fell down and started forming what would later become the Earth. Still, for now, humanity's future home was a shapeless floating mass that was yet to come together among the waters of the ancient ocean. As the chaos organized itself slowly and gradually—the whole process happening over countless ages—numerous gods emerged from the mass. However, there was a problem: The initial world lacked physical objects, so the deities did not have realms to oversee and tasks to perform. Because of this, they hid shortly after they emerged.

Izanagi and Izanami

Among the numerous gods who appeared at that time were Izanagi and Izanami. They were members of the seventh generation of gods and lived in the Heavenly High Plain with their ancestors. However, unlike the other deities, they formed a pair: brother and sister, husband and wife. The older gods told the pair to go down to the floating mass of the Earth and organize it into a firm land.

To complete this monumental task, Izanagi and Izanami needed help. The gods gave them a gift: a spear decorated with jewels called Ama-no-Nuboko. It would serve as a tool to unite all the stubborn particles and solidify them. So, the pair left the heavens. Their task seemed daunting initially because the earth particles were almost indistinguishable from the water particles, all floating in whirlwinds.

Then, Izanagi had an idea: What if they tipped the spear into the waters of the vast ocean and started stirring? It was a good start, so the pair of gods got to work. The waters were very salty, so as Izanagi and Izanami stirred, the salt soon crystallized on the spear. As it fell off the tip and back into the ocean, it started forming an island: *Onogoroshima*, the first island of the Japanese archipelago. There, Izanagi and Izanami decided to create their home and rest together. In the middle of the isle, they raised a pillar called the Heavenly August Pillar.

This monument was essential to Izanagi and Izanami's marriage ceremony. They both stood by it, Izanagi turning to the left and Izanami to the right and walked away in opposite directions to the very corners of the island. Then, they turned back again and walked toward each other as if meeting for the first time.

Upon seeing Izanagi, Izanami exclaimed, "Oh, what a handsome young man is coming my way!"

To this, Izanagi responded, "And what a beautiful maiden I can see!"

Then, they joined their hands in marriage and lived together. After their first night on Earth, Izanami became pregnant. She promised herself that if the child was a boy, she would name him Hiruko.

Unfortunately, the child Izanami gave birth to was malformed and didn't have a single bone in its body. Disgusted, Izanami threw the unfortunate little boy into the sea. This was, however, not the end of his life.

The boy floated on the sea like a jellyfish until he washed ashore on the beach in the isle of Hokkaido. There, a group of Ainu fishermen found him and renamed him Ebisu. The *Ainu* are indigenous people of northern Japan, as well as the area surrounding the Sea of Okhotsk, who had lived there even before the arrival of the Japanese. They have their own unique culture and traditions. Ebisu may have originally been an Ainu god of fishermen who was only later linked with Hiruko from the Japanese myth.

With the help of the fishermen, Ebisu overcame his disability. When he was three years old, his skeleton finally developed, and even though he would have slight problems with walking and be deaf forever, he was now happy and loved. As the patron of fishermen, he became known as the Laughing God. Jellyfish, so similar in body structure to Ebisu's initial state, became his attribute.

In time, Ebisu was numbered among deities known as the Seven Lucky Gods, whose protection could bring wealth and abundance.

Ebisu's patronage became primarily associated with food and bountiful harvests. And so, the history of misfortune and rejection became a story of strength and perseverance.

Unfortunately, Izanagi and Izanami never learned what happened to their firstborn child. In the face of their seeming failure, they turned to the older deities from the heavens to consult with them and learn what went wrong with their marital union.

The Japanese Islands

It seemed that the rules of the universe favored a more patriarchal approach. The older gods explained to Izanagi and Izanami that their first child was malformed because they had greeted each other in the wrong order during their ceremony. A woman shouldn't greet a man first. To fix it, they needed to redo the ritual, but this time, Izanagi would be the first to greet Izanami upon seeing her. The new union gave them healthy, though not entirely human-like, offspring, and they formed the rest of the most important islands in the Japanese archipelago. Awaji, Shikoku, Oki, and Kyushu came first, followed by Tsushima and Honshu. Numerous smaller islands came after the bigger ones.

Having successfully formed the Japanese islands, Izanagi and Izanami finally found themselves in a state of true marital bliss. The time came for them to bring forth more offspring.

After creating the Japanese islands, Izanami would give birth to a number of natural wonders, such as mountains, sea, grass, and others—all of them could be considered *kami* (gods), even if they didn't always take the form of a person.

Finally, the time came for Izanami to try again to create personified gods, a task she was eager to perform after the unlucky birth of Ebisu. The second deity she became pregnant with was Kagutsuchi, the god of fire. Tragically, Izanami's labor this time ended in bad luck even greater than before. The fiery child's body burned its mother from the inside, turning her womb into ash. The pain and injury were too hard to withstand, even for a mighty goddess. In the end, Izanami died.

Izanagi, furious in his grief, snatched little Kagutsuchi and, not minding the heat that radiated from the child's body, cut it into eight pieces and scattered them around the world. Kagutsuchi's mutilated body turned into a multitude of significant volcanoes, creating an innumerable amount of deities.

Izanagi's Journey Through Yomi

Unfortunately, Izanagi's revenge on Kagutsuchi could not bring Izanami back from the dead. A deceased goddess? That was unheard of. In fact, death itself was unheard of at this stage of the world's creation. Izanami was no more; she moved to *Yomi*, the realm of the dead.

Heartbroken, Izanagi was determined to pursue her. He roamed the Earth until he found a large hole in the ground: the entrance to Yomi. He went into a deep cavern. As he walked through the pitch-black corridors, he lost track of time. He didn't know if hours, days, or months had passed before he finally reached a ghastly palace located below the roots of the highest trees and largest mountains.

In the middle of that palace sat Izanami. Death had been cruel to her; Izanagi unveiled her form, only to discover that her corpse had rotted and was a feast for maggots. His once beautiful wife was now a matter of tales of horror.

Izanagi cried out in terror. As soon as Izanami's corpse was unveiled, two new gods arose from her rotting organs: Raijin and

Fujin, the gods of thunder and wind, respectively. Their faces were terrifying; they were demon-like and contorted in grotesque grimaces. Raijin played multiple drums that echoed with thunder, while Fujin held a windbag in his hands that created countless typhoons.

Frightened, Izanagi fled from the gods, and they pursued him relentlessly. When he finally reached the surface of the Earth, he quickly rolled a massive stone over the hole in the ground, trapping Raijin and Fujin in Yomi. The fierce gods would not remain there for long; however, they soon found another way to get to the Earth, and from there, they entered our world with their dangerous thunders and winds.

Because of how they were born, Raijin and Fujin are associated with death. However, both gods can sometimes show a more gentle side, too. Raijin is sometimes depicted as a trickster who can be tamed by a bit of cleverness. Fujin can be frightening as well as fiercely protective. According to a legend, when the Mongols tried to invade Japan in 1274 and 1281, Fujin unleashed mighty typhoons that destroyed the Mongol fleet (McClain, 2002). These winds were later named *kamikaze* ("Divine Wind") to highlight their supernatural nature. We, of course, know this term from a completely different modern context.

Let's now return to Izanagi, who momentarily managed to escape Raijin and Fujin's wrath. He wept as he washed himself in a river flowing close to Yomi's entrance. This was a ritual purification, but it was also a cleansing routine performed after the terrible ordeal he experienced.

As Izanagi was cleansing, something unexpected happened: A beautiful goddess emerged from Izanagi's left eye and stood before her father. It was Amaterasu, the goddess of the sun. Her face was radiant, and her beauty was beyond anything that existed in the universe.

Izanagi didn't get a chance to react to this unexpected arrival. He washed his right eye, and another deity emerged: Tsukuyomi, the god of the moon. At last, when Izanagi washed his nose, a third deity, Susanoo—the god of the seas—appeared.

All three stood before Izanagi. Amaterasu was the firstborn, so she was appointed the queen of the sun and the new ruler of the Plain of High Heaven, making her the most important goddess in the world. Even though they were less in stature, her siblings were also beautiful and powerful. Let's learn more about their nature and deeds.

MEETING THE SHINTO DEITIES

When talking about the first gods in the Plain of High Heaven, I used the term *kami* to mean the same thing as the word *deities*. But in reality, kami is a slightly broader term. It encompasses gods and goddesses, but it also includes any beings that are higher in hierarchy than humans. Their status is somewhere between spirits, gods, and the forces of nature. To simplify it, The deities we are about to meet in this chapter—as well as heroes and *yōkai*, or demons, from the following chapters—can be thought of as kami. They are simply beings, whether they have divine bodies or are the bodies of animals or plants, the elements, or even parts of the landscape.

Kami can be good and evil; they do not have unlimited power or know everything. But the belief in them is the core of Shinto, the exclusively Japanese religion. Like deities in other traditions that worship multiple gods, the kami can respond to prayers, but they are also prone to mistakes. Their nature makes for the uniqueness of the stories that are about to unfold before our eyes.

Shintoism believes in dozens, if not hundreds, of kami with multiple local variants. We will not focus on every one of them on our journey; instead, I urge you to explore their stories independently. As our tale unfolds, we will meet Amaterasu, Tsukuyomi, and Susanoo and learn about their deeds. Strap in as we journey from the High Heavenly Plain to the Earth and beyond.

Amaterasu

The Rising Sun, Amaterasu's symbol, became part of Japanese identity as early as the seventh century C.E. (Dyer, 2014) and is still important today. The Japanese emperors claimed that they descended from the goddess of the sun. Additionally, the three holy imperial emblems—the Eight-Span Mirror, the Grand Jewel, and the Grass-Cutting Sword—are believed to be gifts from Amaterasu that were passed down through generations.

The history behind two of these treasures—the Eight-Span Mirror, or Yata-no-Kagami, and the Grand Jewel, or Yasakani-no-Magatama—is an exciting tale and a core myth connected to Amaterasu. It is said that after an argument with her brother Susanoo, who is notorious for causing trouble, the goddess shut herself in a cave and refused to come out under any circumstances. This was a problem because Amaterasu's absence also meant the absence of the sun itself.

By the time this happened, there were already many more gods and goddesses, and they all wanted the conflict to end and for Amaterasu to show herself again. Their leader was Omoikane, the kami of wisdom, who devised a crafty plan to lure the goddess out of her hideout.

Omoikane hung a lustrous mirror on a tall, blossoming cherry tree. It was large enough to reflect the entire body of a person. Omoikane placed a string of comma-shaped beads along its frame, and the beads flickered with silvery light, drawing attention to the mirror itself. The gods gathered curiously around the crafty mirror, admiring their own reflections. Omoikane, however, told them to disperse and take their positions. Soon, the ritual began.

With solemn words and prayers, ritual candle-burning, and dances, the gods worked themselves up into a religious frenzy. The mirror was the center of the ceremony, hanging below the snowy white cherry blossoms, reflecting the faces of the gods. Nobody knew the true purpose of it yet.

Eventually, one of the goddesses, Ame-no-Uzume, started dancing. She was the patroness of joy and ritual performances, and she fell into a trance. The dance would soon turn lively to frantic as the goddess lifted her skirts, revealing her body to the other gods. This caused the others to laugh uneasily and loudly. It was so loud, in fact, that even Amaterasu heard it from her cave.

That was what Omoikane had been counting on. The sun goddess was curious and slightly envious. What happy celebration were the gods enjoying without her? She called out from her hideout, asking what all the fun was about.

The music and dance stopped abruptly, and the entire High Heavenly Plain stood still. At last, Ame-no-Uzume, still reeling from her dance, dared to speak. She knew Omoikane's plan, so she spoke a previously rehearsed lie. She said that a goddess even greater than Amaterasu had appeared, and all the kami were now celebrating her.

As planned, this crumbled Amaterasu's resolve. She was now curious—and more than a little bit jealous—and she gently pushed the rock blocking the entrance to the cave. From that spot, she had a direct view of the great mirror, so the only thing she could see was her own reflection.

She didn't recognize herself. All she saw was a face of a charming and graceful woman. More and more interested, she stepped out of the cave.

Then, all the gods jumped on her together, binding her, and sealed the entrance to the cave forever. Thanks to Omoikane, Amaterasu —and with her, the sun—would never hide again.

Tsukuyomi

Tsukuyomi, the second-born child of Izanagi's ritual cleansing, is also Amaterasu's husband. As with every well-matched pair, the gods have some things in common while also remaining opposites in other aspects. Like Amaterasu, Tsukuyomi loves order and peace, but he is milder than his wife. While Amaterasu guides the fiery, brilliant sun, Tsukuyomi guards the silver, glowing moon. As the night, he complements and opposes Amaterasu's day.

However, there is also a tragedy to their union: Tsukuyomi always chases Amaterasu, and yet they can never meet. But it was not always like that. Once upon a time, the moon and the sun shared the same sky. The tragedy of the separation between the night and the day came from Tsukuyomi's mistake and an argument that changed the lives of the divine couple forever. It turned the moon god into a figure viewed negatively in the Shinto religion.

One day, Ukemochi, the goddess of food, organized a lavish feast. As the deity of nourishment, she was capable of producing food straight out of her mouth, as well as other orifices in her body. Even though it could seem unpleasant, this process resulted in food that was not only perfectly nourishing but also delicious.

However, for Tsukuyomi, Ukemochi's behavior clearly violated etiquette. When sent to the feast as Amaterasu's representative, he accidentally overlooked the goddess spitting out fish, rice, and other ingredients and shivered, offended.

Tsukuyomi's horror wasn't only the result of disgust, however. As the deity of order, his task was to ensure that proper manners were followed when preparing food. Ukemochi needed to be punished for her misstep. Blinded by rage, Tsukuyomi killed her on the spot. He didn't realize that his behavior created a paradox—to enforce order, he himself broke it.

Amaterasu was furious. She now realized that Tsukuyomi's idea of order was completely different from her own. She couldn't overlook a disagreement over such fundamental values. In her mind, her union with Tsukuyomi was now finished, and she refused to even look at him, banning the moon god from the High Heavenly Plain. So, the night and day were separated, and Tsukuyomi was forever doomed to chase Amaterasu but never reach her.

Susanoo

Susanoo, the third of Izanagi's children, is perhaps even more explosive than the once-impulsive Tsukuyomi. The god of the seas and storms, he can be as violent as the most disruptive of tempests.

From the moment of his birth, Susanoo caused trouble. He destroyed entire forests and killed many with his storms. In the Plain of High Heaven, such behavior was inexcusable. After all, this was a peaceful, glorious kingdom located in the clouds. Finally, the gods grew tired of Susanoo's conduct. After a debate, they decided to banish him from the Heavenly High Plain.

Unsurprisingly, even Susanoo's final departure ended with disruption. He raged, and as he passed by Amaterasu's lavish sunlit palace, he utterly destroyed its surroundings. Pastures and gardens were laid to waste; trees were felled by the wind and flowers were trampled by hail.

When challenged, Susanoo said he was innocent. He said this was just how he was and that the other gods could hardly blame him for his nature. He was even willing to perform a great feat to prove his innocence: He would give birth to new gods, and if they all turned out to be male, that would mean he was telling the truth.

Reluctantly, Amaterasu agreed and sealed the pact. Then, suddenly, Susanoo reached to her neck, snatched her jeweled necklace, and swallowed the precious gems. He then flew down from the High Heavenly Plain. One by one, hundreds of new kami, one made of each jewel, emerged from his body. The new gods were all male, which suggests that Susanoo hadn't lied, at least in his own mind. Later, all the gods he gave birth to would become ancestors of Japanese nobility.

Amaterasu was beyond offended. The theft of her jewels became the offense that caused her to shut herself in the cave from which she would later have to be lured out, as we have already discussed.

After coming to Earth, Susanoo continued his destructive ways. However, despite his violent tendencies, the god's compassionate side came out during his wanderings. He found himself in the Izumo province in Honshu's western region and roamed along the river Hi. There, he heard a faint sound of weeping in the distance. He followed the sound until he found an elderly couple in distress.

Susanoo asked them what was wrong. Through sobs, they managed to explain that a giant serpent dragon called Orochi had just devoured another one of their daughters.

"Another one?" exclaimed Susanoo. "How many of your daughters has he taken?"

"Seven," the old man responded, "The serpent has been a menace for quite some time. Now, we have only one daughter left,

Kushinada-hime, and we don't know what would happen to us if we were to sacrifice her as well."

Susanoo couldn't stand for such injustice. He assured the couple that he would fight Orochi when the monster came to collect his next victim. For that, however, he needed a plan.

He started by ensuring Kushinada-hime's safety. He turned her into a comb with his power and placed her in his hair so the evil serpent couldn't find her. Then, he told the couple to prepare sake—the most potent alcohol they had. When it was ready, they placed eight cups full of it at each entrance to their house.

Soon, Orochi arrived: a giant, monstrous serpent. He had eight heads, and each of them was spitting fire from its nostrils. It was a fearsome sight, even for a god-like Susanoo. But he swallowed his fear and waited for the opportune moment, hidden behind the corner of the house.

Orochi trashed around the house, searching for another maiden to devour. As he did, he smelled the sake—just as Susanoo had predicted. Orochi couldn't resist the strong scent and the promise of a pleasurable drink. He started draining the cups—one for each head. Soon, the mighty dragon became completely drunk and fell into a deep sleep.

That was the moment Susanoo had been waiting for. Jumping from behind the corner of the house, he cut off Orochi's heads one by one. Then, he quartered his body. As he was cutting through Orochi's stomach, Susanoo saw something shining inside. Carefully, he extracted a mighty and extremely sharp sword. This was Kusanagi-no-Tsurugi, the Grass-Cutting Sword, the third attribute of the Japanese imperial family. As a token of his apology to Amaterasu, Susanoo gifted the sword to her. Later, the goddess would pass this inheritance, along with the Grand Jewel and the Eight-Span Mirror, to her descendants.

In the end, the classic story of a hero fighting a dragon for a maiden ended the only way it could: by Susanoo marrying Kushinada-hime and settling down. Still being violent and causing storms, he was no longer uncontrollable. Afterward, He made amends with Amaterasu, bringing the world back into balance.

SACRED SPACES IN MYTHOLOGY

Now that we have met the leading players in Japanese mythology, it is time to stroll through its fantastical locations. Besides the already mentioned Plain of High Heaven and the underworld, there is also *Ashihara no Nakatsukuni*, the human world—or, simply put, the Earth. The universe of the Japanese myth has three parts. So, let's journey from heaven's highest clouds through the underworld's lowest caverns. Perhaps this will make us look at our ordinary plain of existence in a slightly different light!

Takamagahara

As we've discussed, *Takamagahara*, or the Plain of High Heaven, was the first location to emerge from the chaotic particles of the ancient universe. It is the birthplace of the gods. But what does it look like? Should we simply imagine clouds and an abundance of light?

The truth is, old Japanese chronicles don't give us a vivid description of Takamagahara beyond saying that it is the dwelling place of the gods above the heavens. One can only access it through a special heavenly bridge, Ame-no-Ukihashi, which is made either out of the rays in a rainbow or the stars in the Milky Way. Izanagi and Izanami stood on this bridge while stirring the waters and creating the first island of the Japanese archipelago. Only those with pure hearts can access this airy passage.

Some even think that Takamagahara could be a symbolic representation of an actual location on Earth, either in or outside Japan (Tanaka et al., 1998). In this simplified explanation, all the mythological tales would be simply retellings of long-forgotten historical stories. A spiritual narrative, however, suggests that the location of Takamagahara is beyond the confines of the known world: high above the clouds in the sky. A location like this definitely seems more poetic.

Yomi

From the sunny and airy plains of the heavens, we turn to the dark caverns of the underworld—the place of death and decay. There, even a god as mighty as Izanagi stood helpless and stunned in the face of mortality.

Yomi is believed to be located under the surface of the Earth. Its other name, *Ne-no-kuni*, means "Land of Roots." However, getting there from the Earth is not easy, and there are only two entrances. One lies in the province of Izumo, and it is the one that Izanagi used. It is now blocked by a large boulder, a remnant of the god's escape from Yomi. The other is even more difficult to find. It lies at the world's end, where all the seas meet and fall into a giant hole. This is the passage that Raijin and Fujin used when they finally escaped to the Earth.

Besides the myth of Izanagi and Izanami, only one other story mentions Yomi. It was believed that the god Susanoo, after he defeated Orochi and got married, became the new lord of Yomi, building his palace at Yomi's entrance. Different stories say he was either awarded this position willingly or was sent there as punishment for mourning excessively after his mother, Izanami.

No other Japanese myths refer to Yomi. Shintoism as a religion is more focused on life on Earth rather than on what awaits people after death. And so, Yomi became the hidden land—both physically and spiritually.

Ashihara no Nakatsukuni

Finally, *Ashihara no Nakatsukuni*, or the "Central Land of Reed Plains," refers to our familiar Earth. It is the plain where all the heroic and more mundane tales unfold, a place where the *kami* live alongside the people and spirits hide in plain sight. In the following chapters, we will mostly stay on Earth, which is so well-known and yet so mysterious.

As we conclude our exploration of the key gods and goddesses in Japanese mythology, we are opening the door to many more stories. These narratives unfold with deified heroes and everyday individuals entangled in extraordinary tales. Spirits wander through both deserted paths and bustling cities. The divine beings we met in this chapter will continue to shape the following tales— having sculpted the universe and woven the destinies of mortals. Brace yourself for the next phase of our journey, where we encounter heroes whose legacies are forever imprinted on Japanese culture and history.

2

LEGENDARY HEROES AND
HEROINES

We have now stepped down from the airy palaces of the High Heavenly Plain and are standing on the firm ground of Ashihara no Nakatsukuni, our well-known Earth. However, we are not turning from tales of courage, wisdom, bravery, and adventure. Even if the protagonists of the stories we are about to hear in this chapter are not immortal gods and goddesses, they are still mighty heroes and heroines who have shaped Japanese myth, culture, and tradition for generations to come.

We will meet heroes who descended from the gods—as was traditionally believed to be the case with Japanese emperors and empresses—as well as ordinary individuals who, thanks to courage surpassing their station, immortalized their names in the collective consciousness of the Japanese people. These are not merely stories but actual echoes of Japan's most valiant souls. Their example was emulated by the generations of the samurai, and their courage was admired by those who listened to their tales for centuries. I invite you to witness the lives of those who shaped the legends of a whole nation.

THE EMPEROR JIMMU

Our first story transports us to the very beginnings of the Japanese state, as they lay concealed amid legend and mystery. Jimmu is believed to have ruled Japan as the first Emperor in the seventh century B.C.E. His historicity is contested, and with his ancestors consisting almost predominantly of gods and goddesses, he is more of a supernatural hero than a historical figure. However, as we will hopefully soon see, the events that Jimmu took part in or caused can be viewed as an echo of real processes that took place when the Japanese people first settled their archipelago.

In the Japanese mythical tradition, Jimmu's ascension to the throne ends the Age of the Gods and begins the time of mortals. Jimmu himself is a transitional figure, forever upended between the kami and the people—as would be the whole imperial lineage he founded. In fact, for centuries, the Japanese emperors would be considered incarnations of gods on Earth. It was only after World War II that emperor Hirohito was forced to proclaim that he was not, in fact, a living god.

Let's now come back to ancient times, however, and see how Jimmu accomplished his incredible journey from being the descendant of the gods to being the first ruler of Japan.

Through his father, Ugayafukiaezu, Jimmu was the three times great-grandson of the goddess Amaterasu herself. On his mother's side, he was the grandson of Watatsumi, a mythical water dragon. The union between Jimmu's parents was an unusual one. Tamayori-hime was Ugayafukiezu's aunt and had been playing the role of his foster mother before she became his wife.

Despite the peculiarity of their union, the pair produced four healthy sons, the youngest of whom, Hikohohodemi, would later become Emperor Jimmu. The name *Jimmu* itself was only given to our hero posthumously. However, for the clarity of the narrative, I will call him Jimmu throughout our story.

With such illustrious parentage, it is no wonder that Jimmu and his three brothers believed they were destined for great things. However, nobody expected Jimmu to be the leader; after all, he was the youngest.

The boys grew up in Kyushu, where they built a palace at Takachiho. From the moment they were born, their parents instilled in them the belief that their fate was to rule the entirety of Japan. It is no wonder then that when the brothers grew up, they decided to migrate eastward to find a more suitable location from which they could rule the country.

Jimmu's Migration

Itsuse-no-Mikoto, the eldest brother, led the expedition. From Kyushu, the young men took a maritime route through the Seto Inland Sea and toward modern-day Osaka. That was where they encountered their first complications. Upon landing ashore, the brothers met with a local chieftain, Nagasunehiko. The man was strong and had unnaturally long legs. He denied the passage to our heroes, and a battle ensued between him and their forces.

The fight proved disastrous for the brothers. Itsuse was killed by a stray arrow, and his army was entirely defeated. But instead of lamenting their misadventure and turning around, the remaining brothers gathered and discussed their options.

That was when Jimmu's strategic genius first became known. He realized that his army had lost because, during the battle, it was facing eastward toward the sun. This fact had a double meaning— strategic and spiritual. On a strategic level, an army that fought facing the rising sun had a harder time seeing its enemies, blinded by the sun's rays. From a spiritual perspective, facing the goddess Amaterasu straight ahead was an offense to the divine queen and weakened Jimmu's forces.

There was only one conclusion to make: The army had to regroup and move around, so the next time they battled, they would be facing westward. With haste, the heroes' forces returned to their boats, this time under the guidance of the second-eldest brother, Mikeiri-no-Mikoto. They would sail to the other side of the Kii Peninsula, to the Kumano region.

Tragically, however, a storm ensued, caused by the kami who were unwilling for Jimmu and his brothers to succeed. An exceptionally high tide mounted over one of the boats and washed Mikeiri off the deck. Another brother lost his life as he drowned. Now, all who were left were Jimmu and his elder brother, Inahi-no-Mikoto. Inahi, appreciating Jimmu's strategic thinking, ceded the leadership to him.

Finally, Jimmu's forces found the land again. But the moment they went ashore, the inhospitable gods interfered again, and a great mist fell over the region. The army was forced to stop its march and camp on the shore. Soon, they felt sleepiness overcome them: The mist was poisonous. The whole army fell into a stupor.

As the men were sleeping, one of the soldiers, Kumano-no-Takakuraji, had a strange dream. The goddess Amaterasu herself spoke to him, her face too brilliant to look upon. She showed him a nearby barn and said that he should search under the floor of this building; he would find something extraordinary there.

Kumano woke up with a start. The moment he opened his eyes, he saw the barn from his dream. Agitated, he ran inside and lifted one of the planks on the floor. An extraordinary sight greeted him: a glint of an extremely sharp blade. This was no other sword than Kusanagi-no-Tsurugi, the blade that Susanoo had found inside the body of Orochi and then gifted to Amaterasu.

Kumano ran outside, the sword in his hand. The blade shone beautifully, and its luster caused the mist to disperse. The army started waking up, and Kumano walked toward Jimmu, his leader, and presented the blade to him. Thus, the future Emperor received his first emblem.

This momentary victory didn't mean that the adverse deities gave up on their quest to interfere with Jimmu's march. The region that his army now entered was hard to navigate. Even with Jimmu's wisdom, the army could get lost in the wilderness.

That was when Amaterasu intervened for the second time. She sent a messenger—a three-legged crow by the name of Yatagarasu. The supernatural creature guided Jimmu's army safely toward the plain of Yamato. From time to time, when passing the mountain ranges and walking through forests, Jimmu's army would engage in small fights with the local people whom they called the Emishi. It was an ethnic group distinct from the Japanese and probably related to the Ainu. The word *Emishi* itself is an uncharitable descriptor meaning "shrimp barbarians"—a derogatory term used by the Japanese to refer to a group of people they had been trying to conquer for generations.

When Jimmu's forces finally reached Yamato, they fought with Nagasunehiko again. However, before the battle, the chieftain came to Jimmu's camp, in an attempt to persuade him against the fight. He said he had sworn allegiance to a descendant of the gods, and this illustrious kami would be furious if Jimmu conquered his land. This was no surprise to the future Emperor; after all, adversary forces had been trying to impede his army's march for a long time.

"If you are sworn to this kami, you need to prove it," Jimmu told Nagasunehiko.

"Certainly," the chieftain responded. Then, he lifted his robes and presented Jimmu with an arrow and a quiver.

Our hero immediately recognized divine craftsmanship. However, he possessed a similar arrow and a quiver, also made by the gods, gifted to his brothers, and later to him by his parents. He now unveiled his legacy, and Nagasunehiko immediately realized that he had been put in an impossible situation: to choose between allegiance to two descendants of the gods.

The battle was inevitable. As Jimmu's forces were now facing westward, their victory was assured. Nagasunehiko's forces dispersed, and the chieftain was executed. Nagasunehiko's comrade-in-arms and vassal, Nigihayahi, swore allegiance to Jimmu.

Now, nothing stood between our hero and his ascension to the Japanese imperial throne.

A day after his coronation, Jimmu scaled a sacred mountain, Mount Unebi, in Nara Prefecture. From there, he wished to survey his newly conquered land. He now controlled the entirety of the Seto Inland Sea and the regions surrounding it.

The view from the mountain was spectacular: peaceful green plains and blueish mountains in the distance, all under a clear sky. In the shining sun, the shape of the land resembled a heart or a very characteristic shape that two dragonflies would make when mating. This fact was not lost on Jimmu, who commented upon it. The word that he used, *akitsu*, in archaic Japanese, meant "dragonfly." So, for centuries, Japan's customary name became Akitsushima, the Dragonfly Islands.

According to the legend, Jimmu's reign lasted for 76 years and was very peaceful. The Emperor died at a ripe old age of 126. He was buried near Mount Unebi.

Jimmu's story is that of aggression and conquest, which was given a supernatural explanation to justify its necessity. Even if full of supernatural events, it most likely reflects some truth about the historical migrations of the Japanese. Jimmu's cult as a deity and ancestor of all emperors was present in Japanese culture for generations. Still, it became especially pronounced in the second part of the 19th century when the rule of the Emperor was restored and strengthened under Emperor Meiji (Saaler, 2016).

YAMATO TAKERU—THE PRINCE OF ADVENTURE

The story of Yamato Takeru is a tale of how courage was coupled with cunning in the form of one clever and courageous individual. Yamato was a legendary prince, a member of the imperial family of Yamato, believed to have lived in the second century C.E. He was the son of the 12th Emperor and a descendant of Jimmu. His story was written down in the two core Japanese chronicles, the *Kojiki* and *Nihon Shoki*.

Yamato Takeru's name was not one that he was given upon his birth but, rather, an epithet he received on one of his adventures. Instead, the child had been named Yamato Ousu.

From the moment the royal child was born, it was clear that the boy would become someone extraordinary. As he grew, Ousu showed nearly supernatural bouts of strength, all the while possessing the countenance of a beautiful boy. The radiance of his face matched that of graceful maidens, but his power and impulsiveness immediately announced his virility. Unfortunately, this combination would both bring him fame and misfortune.

In Ousu's adolescence, bad luck struck for the first time. While being tasked with reprimanding his brother for a minor misstep, the young hero underestimated the strength of his muscles and accidentally tore the limbs off the other boy's body, killing him instantly. His father, Emperor Keikō, refused to believe Ousu's tearful explanation—instead, he feared the youth's violent tendencies, distrust sown in his heart forever.

However, an emperor who is afraid of his own son cannot have the son assassinated upon the pain of disgrace. There were other ways of possibly sending Ousu to his death under the guise of a difficult and responsible diplomatic mission. So, the Emperor tasked his son with single-handedly subjugating a rebellious tribe of the Kumasu—mythical people living on the isle of Kyushu.

The Subjugation of Kumasu

Ousu realized that the task before him was difficult, if not impossible, to accomplish alone. Yet, he also knew that he couldn't bear to stay in his father's presence. Fortunately, not all the members of the royal court had turned away from young Ousu: His aunt, Princess Yamatohime, a wise and pious woman who had established a large and famous shrine of the goddess Amaterasu in Ise, was determined to help her nephew.

Despite his mighty strength, Ousu couldn't subdue an entire tribe of rebels alone; he had to devise a clever ruse instead. For this purpose, Yamatohime gifted him her skirt and outer garments. Ousu put on his aunt's clothes and let his hair down in a womanly fashion. The garments concealed his lithe, male form; combined with his beautiful face, he now looked like a young noblewoman.

Before Ousu embarked on his journey, Yamatohime introduced him to a beautiful young lady. This was Ototachibana, who

JAPANESE MYTHOLOGY UNLEASHED | 37

became Ousu's wife that very night. In the morning, fortified by a newfound love, Ousu began his quest to the land of the Kumasu.

Disguised, Ousu penetrated the camp of the Kumasu. A graceful maiden wearing rich garments instantly sparked the attention of the bandits' leader, Torishi-kaya. No threat was perceived to come from an unassuming young woman, so Ousu wasn't searched for weapons. He concealed his sword under the vast, flowing robes.

Torishi-kaya, attracted to Ousu's beauty, invited him to a feast to sit by his side. Small talk was exchanged, food was distributed among the guests, and drinks flowed freely. As time passed, more and more attendants became drunk. But Ousu kept his wits, feigning female modesty and refusing to partake in alcohol too much. Finally, however, he saw his moment arrive: The guests were now almost entirely drunk, and Torishi-kaya was doing no better. Ousu reached under his robes, took out his sword, and stabbed the rebel right through his heart.

The enemies, alarmed and woken from their drunken stupor, scrambled to their feet but were in no condition to fight Ousu. Torishi-kaya let out a rattling breath. He was not dead yet, and Ousu was about to twist the blade in his body and finish the job— but the rebel raised his hand, begging the prince to stop. Ousu hesitated, and that moment was enough for Torishi-kaya to speak some momentous words. "You have behaved very cleverly, young man," he said. "Can you now reveal your real name?"

Ousu nodded. "My name is Yamato Ousu, and I am the son of Emperor Keikō," he responded.

Tarishi-kaya closed his eyes briefly, then continued speaking in between labored breaths. "I am the strongest man in my land, and I have met many brave men, yet I have bested them all. However, nobody matched your cleverness and might, Prince Ousu. As my dying wish, would you accept a new name for yourself? For even though it is uttered from a rebel's disgraced mouth, it is worthy of your deed today."

Ousu nodded again. "Say the name, then."

"It will be Yamato Takeru, the Brave of Yamato."

Ousu smiled. "I will accept this name."

With that, Torishi-kaya let out his last breath.

The defeat of the rebels' leader meant the subjugation of the entire tribe. Now, under a new name, Yamato Takeru traveled back to his father in glory. He hoped that his clever and courageous deed would help clear his name before the Emperor.

However, it was not meant to be. If anything, Emperor Keikō was now even more afraid of his son as the word of his accomplishments spread far and wide. So, immediately upon Takeru's return, the Emperor devised another mission to send him on.

The Eastern Rebels

This time, the mission was even more difficult than the last. Takeru's task was not only to subjugate another group of rebels but also to tame unruly lesser kami and demons who resided in the far-away mountain range to the east. The quest was deemed too dangerous to warrant anyone else's involvement, so Takeru was ordered to embark on a new journey.

Takeru bemoaned his fate. He now fully realized that his father was most likely trying to cause his death. Yet again, our hero met with his aunt Yamatohime, opening his heart before her. This time, she could no longer help him, he said; he was probably riding to meet his end.

Yamatohime sighed and bid Takeru wait. Then, she walked to her treasury and retrieved a large wooden chest. When she opened it, light shone out, and Takeru's eyes widened with awe. Inside the chest lay Kusanagi-no-Tsurugi, the blade of Susanoo and Emperor Jimmu. Now, it was time for Takeru to take it.

Our hero thanked his aunt profusely. Now, his chances of victory were much higher. He set out on his journey, and this time, his wife Ototachibana accompanied him and took an active part in his adventures.

Many perils were waiting for Takeru on his quest. First, he and Ototachibana arrived on the shores of the Suruga province on the island of Honshu. Takeru descended upon the land and wandered the nearby moors, searching for potential rebels to subdue. He interrogated some locals who claimed they hadn't seen any rebels; however, recognizing a great warrior in Takeru, they told him that a hunting party was gathering nearby. Deer were abundant in Suruga, and it would be an honor if Takeru joined the hunters.

What our hero was not aware of, however, was that the people he had spoken to were themselves the rebellious brigands. They recognized an imperial emissary in Takeru and decided to create a ruse. They would wait until the prince was out in the moors, away from any human settlement, and they would set fire to the grassland. It was a foolproof plan: The grass would catch fire immediately, and Takeru, despite his strength, would have no way of defending himself against the power of nature itself.

Initially, everything went according to the bandits' plan. Our hero set out on the hunt early in the morning. He wandered for some time through the grassland, focusing on spotting deer; it was too late when he realized all the members of his hunting party suddenly vanished. Before he could even call out after them, he saw fire rapidly spreading over the moors. It was coming from all directions; there was no escape.

However, what the brigands didn't consider was Takeru's hidden weapon: the sword Kusanagi. Our hero, quick on his feet, unsheathed the blade and started cutting at the grass that had already caught fire. As the sword was extremely sharp and fast to swing about, Takeru could cut his way through the moors and out into safety. And thus, the blade's name was forged: the Grass-Cutting Sword.

Angered, Takeru went back to the brigand's camp. There, he created a bloodbath for his would-be assassins, entirely quenching the rebellion in the province.

Now, Takeru and Ototachibana traveled to other parts of Honshu by sea, through what today constitutes Tokyo Bay. The pair wanted to reach the settlements of the Emishi people.

As Takeru and Ototachibana sailed, the sea was raging. Susanoo, Raijin, and Fujin played their tempestuous orchestra of thunder, lightning, and typhoons. It soon became evident that the only way to assuage the anger of the gods would be to sacrifice a member of Takeru's party.

Since Takeru and Ototachibana traveled alone, the choice was only between them. Then, out of love for Takeru and the wish for his quest to succeed, Ototachibana volunteered to sacrifice herself. There was nothing Takeru could do; she stepped out of the boat's edge and jumped in between the roaring waves.

Long did Takeru look after his lost wife, crying as he felt the sea calming and the winds subsiding almost immediately after she drowned. Her sacrifice, at least, was not in vain. When the boat was finally moored, and Takeru descended upon the beach, he noticed a comb washing ashore. He immediately recognized it as belonging to his wife and wept again; then, he built a little shrine around it.

Meanwhile, the Emishi people gathered on the shore. Realizing they had encountered a prince, they immediately surrendered and allowed him to capture their chieftains. Takeru could now return to his father, the Emperor, to once again prove to him that he was an obedient son.

Later Adventures and Downfall

This time, however, Takeru was not fated to return to his father. Having learned from his earlier misfortune, he traveled back to the capital by land, but he lost his way in the mountains in the central region of Honshu. Wandering in circles, depleting his food resources, and slowly losing his strength, Takeru was almost devoid of hope when suddenly, he saw a beautiful maiden standing on his path.

This was Miyazu-hime from an old noble Owari clan. Still mourning his late wife, Takeru longed nonetheless for a relationship with a woman. At that moment, he mostly wished for a hot meal and a place to stay. Miyazu-hime provided him with just that.

She led him to her dwelling place: the Atsuta Shrine, which she guarded. There, Takeru rested, assured in the promise of being guided on his subsequent journey. However, he wasn't immune to Miyazu-hime's charms and still remembered what awaited him in the capital. Would his father truly change his mind and finally embrace his valiant son? Or, would he continue to send him on dangerous missions until his death? Was it even worth it to come back and find out?

An impulsive decision seemed the only right one at the moment: Takeru would marry Miyazu-hime and dwell with her in her shrine. It would be a much simpler life than the one he had led to this point. It wouldn't lack in adventures, either. Miyazu-hime had informed her new husband that a multitude of demons were hiding in the mountains, and a hero who would subdue them would be a true savior of the entire region.

So, Takeru's new life began. He would set out numerous times to fight demonic kami, who took on various forms. Every time, he would take his sword, Kusanagi, with him, and every time he would win. This string of victories made him boastful, verging on arrogance. Finally, one day, he decided to fight the god of the nearby summit, Mount Ibuki, himself. Not only that, but he also vowed he would take this foe on empty-handed. So, he left Kusanagi behind in the care of Miyazu-hime.

As Takeru traveled through the wilderness, he spotted a large white deer in the distance. The animal seemed supernaturally big; there was something eerie about it. From time to time, it even seemed to change into a white serpent, only to revert in moments to its previous form. It could simply be Takeru's mind playing tricks on him, but he decided to take this sight as a sign. This must be the god's messenger, he reasoned. He decided to approach and kill it.

He didn't realize that the god himself had become the deer-serpent. When Takeru jumped on the animal's back and wrestled it, he quickly realized the creature was too strong even for him. It wounded him with one of his horns, escaped his grasp, and ran away.

Even though wounded, Takeru could still walk, and hobbling, he returned to his wife's house. On his way, however, the god of Mount Ibuki unleashed an icy storm. A chill settled in Takeru's bones, an illness that was beyond an ordinary fever. The god had cursed him, and he would now die slowly and in pain.

Takeru realized what was happening. Trembling, he arrived at his new home, where he said goodbye to Miyazu-hime and asked her to give him back his sword. Then, he set out on a doomed journey to the capital. Unsurprisingly, he didn't manage to reach it before his death. When he arrived at the Nobono Shrine in Kameyama, he drew his last breath.

The news about Takeru's death traveled far and wide and soon reached the ears of the Emperor himself. Tragically, it was only then that Keikō realized his son's courage and devotion. Heartbroken, he ordered a mausoleum to be constructed on the site of Nobono Shrine. When the construction was finished and Takeru's coffin placed on a dais, a large white bird was spotted sitting on the mausoleum's ramparts. Before anyone was able to capture it, it flew away in the direction of the capital.

The curious onlookers opened Takeru's coffin then. It was empty; only the hero's clothing remained inside. This clearly showed that Yamato Takeru had been turned into a kami. His memory remained among the people and, in time, turned into a cult. Under the name Otori-sama, "The Great Bird," Takeru is worshipped to this day in various shrines across Japan. His feast is held in early November when he is evoked as a patron of prosperity. The character of Yamato Takeru inspired novels, anime series, and video games. The story of a boy wielding a magical sword has been reworked in the Japanese *Yamato Takeru* series (1994) and compared to the legend of King Arthur by Western scholars (Littleton, 1995). The ancient hero lives on in the imagination of the people from Japan and beyond.

EMPRESS JINGU—THE CONQUERING HEROINE

So far, the strongest female character we have encountered in our mythological tales was Amaterasu. Even though we met a number of interesting women whose wisdom and courage often helped male heroes on their adventures, we have also seen that despite this fact, traditional Japanese culture was inherently patriarchal—as seen in the story of Izanagi and Izanami's marriage ceremony. But from time to time, a strong-willed woman would emerge and challenge the rule of men. One of those women was Empress Jingu, a semi-legendary ruler whose reign started on the cusp of the third century C.E.

Jingu was a wife and consort of Chuai, the 14th Emperor of the Japanese. As the queen, Jingu's duty was to lead spiritual rituals and engage in acts of divination on behalf of her people. She was a supreme shamaness, so exemplary that she became a symbol and an ideal to emulate for all queens after her. Jingu ruled in a truly equal partnership with her husband. While he conducted military and administrative affairs on Earth, she was a diplomat between the Earth and the High Heavenly Plain. It was an arguably even more critical role.

However, Jingu wanted to rule over all. She was trained not only in spiritual matters but also in martial arts. She was an *onna-musha* —a woman warrior who could fight in battles alongside the samurai (DeMarco, 2016). She accompanied her husband, the Emperor, on his military campaigns, aiding him both by acts of her divination as well as her martial skills.

Emperor Chuai didn't lack enemies. He was the son of the famous Yamato Takeru, and he still had to deal with the Kumasu people, whom his father had temporarily subdued. That enemy, however, wasn't dangerous enough to threaten the sovereignty of the

Japanese Yamato kingdom. Still, Jingu stayed by her husband's side as he set out to fight.

As was the custom, Chuai asked his wife to be brought into a trance and communicate the gods' will as to his next moves against the Kumasu. The military chieftains then gathered around the fire, surrounding the Empress. A shaman started playing a stringed instrument, and the melody slowly transported Jingu to another plane of existence. Soon, with her head thrown back and her eyes half-closed, she communicated the message from the spirits: The Emperor had to cease his attempts to conquer the Kumasu and instead turn his sight over the sea toward the Korean kingdom of Silla. It was a rich land full of treasures of all kinds. There was a chance that Chuai could subdue this kingdom without bloodshed —if he agreed to worship the spirit that conveyed the message.

The Emperor grew angry. He was a stubborn man, and hearing the words of the spirits contradicting his will displeased him. He reached to his wife and shook her out of the trance. Still bewildered by her supernatural experience, Jingu now had to listen to Chuai's shouting and accusations of fabricating the whole message. She narrowed her eyes. How dare her husband accuse her of lying when it came to matters of the spirits?

"Perhaps you didn't lie," Chuai said, "But that spirit must have. It was probably a demon."

Jingu's anger grew. She was the supreme shamaness; she could distinguish between a benevolent spirit and a demon. She demanded to be put into a trance again.

And again, the spirit repeated its message—this time more angrily and insistently. The kingdom of Silla had to be conquered, but Chuai would now never see it happen during his lifetime. This message exacerbated the Emperor's anger, and he left the divination circle, intent on disregarding his wife and riding out to battle against the Kumasu.

Soon, the spirit's words proved true: Chuai was killed during the battle. He and Jingu didn't have any born heirs, so the dynasty was likely to fall apart. The Empress knew that she had to assume the throne and consolidate her power, shutting the mouths of those who would deny the throne to a woman.

To achieve that, however, she needed more time. She decided to keep Chuai's death a secret for a bit longer. During that time, she spiritually purified herself and entered a religious trance again. She sought to find the spirits who had spoken to her before, and when she did, she asked them for precise instructions.

The to-do list went like this: Jingu was to send one of her generals against the Kumasu, while she herself had to prepare for the conquest of Korea. This would take her three years, during which the spirits would protect her. The kami revealed that the Empress had been pregnant at the time of her husband's death. Through divine power, the spirits would ensure that the pregnancy would last three full years, giving Jingu enough time to complete her military campaign.

Jingu came out of her trance with a newfound sense of purpose. She sent envoys to shrines that worshipped the spirits she had communed with, and she ordered one of her generals to set out against the Kumasu. Because the campaign was led this time while honoring the spirits' will, a swift victory over the rebels ensued. Jingu could now sleep peacefully as the reigning Empress, preparing for her conquest.

Conquest of Korea

Soon, Jingu's troops were recruited and gathered at a beach near the battleships. The soldiers cheered as the Empress went out to salute them, dressed in warrior garb, a large battle axe in her hand.

Jingu raised her hand and quieted the crowd. She then spoke to her soldiers, urging them to be swift and effective but not unnecessarily cruel. She reiterated the words that the spirits had uttered about the divine justification of the conquest.

As a margin note, it is worth noticing here how the Japanese narrative reinforces the idea that the conquest of Korea was the right endeavor to undertake. Today, of course, this is a controversial topic. The Korean point of view on these matters is, unsurprisingly, wildly different.

Let's come back to the mythical narrative, however—and more specifically, to the night before the departure of the troops. Jingu couldn't sleep that night. Tossing and turning, she was thinking about the words of the spirits who, yet again, spoke to her. She was assured of victory but hoped that any adverse tides wouldn't shipwreck her fleet on the sea. The ocean was an unpredictable place, the domain of wild Susanoo, Raijin, Fujin, and a number of dragon monsters.

Suddenly, the door to Jingu's cabin opened, and a figure appeared in the doorway. Jingu sat up, startled. The stranger unveiled himself, showing a radiant, god-like countenance. It was Azumi-no-isora, a minor kami of the seashore. He said he had a gift for the Empress that would help her control the tides. He would give it to her if she agreed to spend a night with him.

Jingu shook her head. "I cannot," she said. "I am pregnant with the future Emperor."

Just then, a tiny voice could be heard coming from the direction of Jingu's womb. It was the yet unborn child, miraculously speaking to his mother and agreeing for her to have intercourse if it meant victory in her future campaign.

So, Jingu relented. She spent the night with Azumi-no-isora, and when the dawn came, the god disappeared, leaving two stones on the Empress's bedside.

Those were the tide jewels. They could bring about high or low tide at will. So, Jingu's fleet sailed, and the Empress strapped the stones to her stomach, directing the fleet in a way that it arrived at Korean shores at a time when nobody would have expected it. The Japanese army marched to the capital of Silla completely unhindered. In the capital, the king and his entire court submitted to Jingu immediately, and she accepted his surrender, preventing her soldiers from killing him.

As the spirits promised, Jingu returned to Japan after three years, all the while carrying her supernaturally long pregnancy. Upon her return, she fought another battle, defeating the crown's enemies and ensuring her unborn son's succession. Then, and only then, could she settle down and finally give birth to Ojin.

She continued to rule in her son's stead not only during his childhood but also into adulthood. She refused to give up her throne until Ojin was 70 years old. During her reign, she held power over the kingdom of Silla and later also subjugated another Korean realm, Paekche. Her reign marked an era of Japanese prosperity.

Yet again, it is worth stressing that the narrative of Jingu is, at its heart, a militaristic tale, propagating the Japanese right to Korean sovereignty. However, it is also a tale of a strong woman who communed with the gods, who was wiser than her husband and more powerful than her son, and who managed to assume both traditional female and male roles in the ancient society of Japan.

THE PEACH BOY AND THE FISHER LAD

With the story of the Peach Boy and the Fisher Lad, we are moving away from tales taking place in a semi-legendary and yet assumed historical period. We will no longer focus on empresses and princes; instead, we will listen to tales of ordinary people, ones that took place "once upon a time" rather than in a tangible era and location. Let's see how these unassuming characters get entangled in extraordinary events and how they rise to fame or meet their tragic end.

Momotaro

The story of Momotaro, or the Peach Boy, starts like many folktales do: Once upon a time, there was an elderly couple who didn't have any children. By the time our tale begins, the pair had already resigned to this fact, but they were still worried that nobody would take care of them in their old age.

One day, however, the old woman was doing her laundry by a nearby stream. That was when she noticed a large peach floating on the water's surface. It was larger than any peach she had seen before. Quickly, she snatched it; food was scarce for her and her husband.

When the woman brought the peach home and put it on her kitchen table, something extraordinary happened. As the couple cut the fruit open to share it between themselves, they discovered a sleeping baby inside. It was a little boy, and he looked like an ordinary, healthy child. For a long time, the couple discussed what they should do with the boy. Finally, they decided that he had been their long-awaited gift from the gods. They named him Momotaro ("Peach Boy") and decided to raise him as their own.

The child grew healthy and strong and gave much joy to his adoptive parents. From an early age, Momotaro was aware of where he had come from and was grateful that the old couple had taken him in. By the time he was 15, he decided he needed to repay them for their kindness.

As it happened, the neighborhood in which Momotaro lived was not entirely peaceful. On a nearby island, a group of *oni* had constructed a stronghold and would occasionally raid the neighboring villages. Who were the oni? In Japanese mythology, this is a type of demon, slightly resembling an ogre or a troll in appearance, who would often live in mountain caves. They can sometimes provide good fortune to people, but most of the time, they are dangerous. The particular group of oni who lived near Momotaro's village would mainly occupy themselves with stealing the villagers' treasure and kidnapping their wives.

Having created a goal for himself, Momotaro went home to ask his parents' permission for the trip. Predictably, the old couple wasn't thrilled by the boy's plan and asked him to reconsider. But Momotaro was relentless. He felt it was only fitting for him to change the neighborhood that had adopted and raised him for the better. Seeing that he could not be persuaded otherwise, the couple gave Momotaro their blessing. His adoptive mother prepared dumplings for his journey, and soon, the boy was off on his quest for courage and fame.

For a while, Momotaro walked alone through a forest. But as he neared the border of his village, a stray dog started following him, lured by the smell of the delicious dumplings. This was no ordinary dog: It could speak. It asked Momotaro about the contents of his bag and the purpose of his journey. The boy explained patiently.

"I can help you on your quest if you give me one of your dumplings," offered the dog.

Momotaro agreed. They stopped for a brief snack break, after which they continued on their journey.

They didn't stay alone for long. Soon, a talking monkey jumped from a tree above them. This animal could also speak, and it offered its help in exchange for another dumpling. And then, a third creature, a pheasant, appeared and did the same. Momotaro now truly had a fellowship of adventurers.

The combined strengths of the three animals helped Momotaro immensely on his quest. As he ambushed the oni stronghold, the pheasant flew above the unsuspecting demons and pecked at their heads from above. The dog, in its turn, ran between the monsters' legs, too fast to be caught, and bit at their calves. Lastly, the monkey jumped around, eluding its pursuers and escaping moments before the oni's blows landed; this tired and angered the demons.

Amidst all this chaos was Momotaro, fighting valiantly. He was physically weaker than the oni, but fortunately, much faster. As he found himself face-to-face with an oni chief, he managed to elude his blows and deal him many cuts with his knife, finally wearing the demon down and killing him in the end.

Seeing the death of their chieftain, the rest of the oni fled in terror. The stronghold was now empty. The four companions opened all the vaults and dungeons, only to discover heaps upon heaps of treasure, as well as a group of terrified women who had been taken captive by the demons.

Momotaro's march back to his village was triumphant. Accompanied by his animal friends and the grateful women, he was carrying gold, jewels, and food. It was a joyous day not only for our hero but also for the whole community that raised him. As his adoptive parents saw him coming back in glory, they shed happy tears.

Urashima Taro

Where the tale of Momotaro is a story of triumph and happy endings, that of Urashima Taro has a considerably more tragic outcome. Let's now dive into a story of a boy whose kindness earned him a reward—and of a divine reward that proved detrimental for a mortal.

Urashima Taro was a young fisherman. Every day, he walked down to the beach and jumped on his little boat, just as his father had done before him. He was a kind boy with a mild disposition. His strength didn't lie in his muscles or bravery but in his empathy. Despite relying on fish for survival, he never killed more than he needed, and he displayed no cruelty toward animals. Instead, he lived in harmony with nature.

One day, as Urashima returned from a long day of work, he spotted a group of boys on the beach. They were all gathered in a circle, bending over something on the ground and laughing in a way that made Urashima uneasy. Having decided to investigate, the young fisherman approached the boys.

When he came closer, he noticed that the object of the boys' interest was a tortoise. The cruel boys were tormenting the poor animal, tugging at its legs, poking it with a stick, and even throwing stones at it. Instantly, Urashima decided to intervene.

"Stop it!" he cried. "That animal did nothing wrong to you, and if you continue to taunt it, it will die!"

The boys laughed even harder and continued to torment the tortoise. For them, it was all good fun.

"Listen," Urashima spoke again, "I can give you some money in exchange for the animal."

That sparked the boys' interest. The leader of the group picked up the tortoise from the ground and held it out in his hands. Urashima, in his turn, took the money out of his pocket.

Once the transaction was complete, Urashima took the tortoise back to the sea. He cooed over it, assuring the animal that it was now safe. Then, he released it into the water.

The story would have ended here, but the tortoise Urashima had saved was not an ordinary animal. A few days later, as Urashima was fishing in his boat, he suddenly heard a voice calling his name. He looked around, alarmed, but could see no man or a woman drowning in the sea. When he looked closer, he noticed a tortoise swimming around his boat.

"I didn't know you could speak!" Urashima exclaimed.

"I can," the tortoise said. "But I am not the same tortoise you had saved. I am a servant of the great Dragon King living in the sea, and I'd like to take you to his palace as a thank you for rescuing someone very dear to him."

"A palace of the Dragon King?" Urashima asked in wonder. "But it must be under the water's surface. I cannot breathe underwater."

"It is indeed at the bottom of the ocean," the tortoise confirmed. "But if you jump on my back, I can take you there without any issue."

Suddenly, the tortoise seemed to grow. Soon, its shell was large enough to fit Urashima. The boy, dazed, hopped onto it. He was excited to see the hidden wonder of an underwater palace.

The journey was shorter than expected. Urashima, submerged in an air bubble, wondered at the marvels he could see on his way: the silverfish, jellyfish, starfish, the algae and corals, and all manners of extraordinary creatures he had never laid eyes on. But nothing could compare to the sight of the palace, with its sloping roofs and silver walls.

At the gate, the tortoise spoke to a giant silverfish, announcing his arrival. Soon, the door opened with a crack, and Urashima saw a multitude of underwater creatures, all greeting him with wonder and joy. To them, a human boy was a true novelty, and they thanked the tortoise for bringing him.

Urashima was dazed by all the wonders he could see and followed his guide. It soon turned out that the crowd of underwater creatures was only a prelude to the real wonder: They parted, and Urashima saw the most beautiful woman he had ever seen. She was clad in blue and green robes, with jewels adoring her neck and her hair flowing freely around her in the water. This was Otohime, the princess of the place and the daughter of the Dragon King.

"Welcome, Urashima Taro," she spoke, her voice like honey. "I want to thank you for your service. It was me who was the tortoise you saved. I welcome you to my palace."

Urashima blinked, dazed. He would have never suspected he could meet an actual princess, not to mention such an extraordinary one. She was not only welcoming him to her palace, but she also continued, stating that he could now become her husband and live in the place of wonder forever. Urashima agreed readily, enchanted with the beauty of the princess.

A marital procession formed. Fish stood adorned in ceremonial garb, and Otohime's garments seemed to shimmer even more in the otherworldly, watery glow. The couple exchanged vows and joined in marriage.

It was then time for a lavish feast. Urashima partook of a multitude of colorful dishes, even though he didn't recognize half of the ingredients. He drank underwater sake, talked to his new subjects, and admired the beauty of his new wife. He roamed the palace grounds. Magically, it was the place where he could experience all four seasons at once, looking at trees blooming with new flowers and withering in the winter air. His new home truly had everything Urashima could have wished for.

The next three days passed in a daze. Between the pleasures of a newlywed and exploring the grand palace, Urashima had little time to think of home. On the third morning, though, he suddenly awoke with a heavy heart. He remembered his life from before he came to the magical kingdom and the parents that he supported. Anxiety pinched his heart: His parents must be so worried about him!

Urashima dressed and spoke to Otohime. He explained the situation and asked if he could return to the surface and visit his parents. When the princess heard the words, her beautiful face contorted with sadness. She started crying.

"What is the matter?" Urashima asked, concerned. "Have I offended you?"

"No, no," she said. "But what you requested saddens me. I can grant you your wish but on one condition."

She produced a small wooden box. "Promise me to take it with you and to never open it, no matter what you see when you arrive at the shore."

Urashima agreed readily. This seemed like an easy request to fulfill. Otohime called for her tortoise servant, and in a blink, the young fisherman was traveling back to Earth, the same way he had arrived at the underwater palace.

When he finally washed ashore, Urashima ran to his parents' house as fast as he could. He only barely registered that the path he took seemed slightly different than usual; some of the trees were taller, and some houses were no longer there. In his haste, Urashima didn't pay it a lot of mind.

He knocked at the door to his house. When it opened, the young man saw a stranger come out. Urashima asked about his father and mother, but the stranger had never heard of them. This was peculiar, but maybe Urashima's parents had moved in the past three days. So, the boy walked from house to house, asking about them.

Nobody had heard of his parents. Slowly, Urashima started feeling as if he was in some terrible dream. Finally, he approached a man who was passing down the street, carrying luggage.

"Excuse me," he said. "My name is Urashima Taro. I'm looking for my—"

But before he could finish, the man dropped his luggage and exclaimed:

"You are Urashima Taro? Don't be ridiculous."

Urashima frowned. "What is ridiculous in that? That's my name."

"You cannot be impersonating a legend."

"A legend? I don't understand."

The man shook his head. "Maybe you're not from here." Then, he started explaining: Some 300 years ago, there had been a man in this village by the name of Urashima Taro. One day, he disappeared into the sea and never came back. The story was practically a legend at this point.

Cold sweat appeared on Urashima's forehead as he understood his situation. The time in the underwater palace passed differently. Each day was like 100 years on Earth. He was now quite literally a man coming back from the dead.

In a daze, Urashima walked back to the beach. He had lost everything: his family and his home. He didn't know how to go back to the underwater kingdom. So, this was how he was being repaid for his kindness?

He reached into his pocket and found the wooden box that Otohime had given him. He remembered her warning, but he was also overtaken with sadness. Surely, there was something inside the box that could help him?

Slowly, he opened the lid.

It was empty—or almost empty. Urashima thought that he felt a mist wash over him as he peered inside. For a moment, nothing happened, but then, suddenly, the fisherman felt great tiredness in his bones. He dropped the box. All his true years were catching up to him in one instant. From a young man, he turned into a middle-aged one, then into an elderly gentleman, then grew older and older—until his bones cracked, skin peeled off his face, and he dropped to the ground, dead.

Urashima's story is a true tragedy. Through one act of curiosity and disobedience, he lost all that he could have had. But more importantly, his act of kindness brought about completely unexpected consequences. This tale illustrates how the world of the gods and the mortals can never truly intersect.

ECHOES IN THE SAMURAI ETHOS

The stories in this chapter have shaped the imagination of the Japanese people, noble and commoner alike, for generations. But there was a particular social group for whom the tales of human bravery provided a model for behavior. Those were the famous samurai, and we can see echoes of the heroic tales in some of the precepts included in their code of conduct, known as the *bushido*. Stories such as the one about Yamato Takeru shaped the early ideal of a warrior: Devoted to his sword, loyal to his family even in adversity, fierce in combat, but also exhibiting emotions such as sadness or distress. Those qualities would be reinforced in later stories, especially the classic Japanese novels such as *The Tale of the Heike* (before 1330) and *The Tale of Genji* (11th century) (McAlpine et al., 1989). Countless other works of art would depict the samurai, creating a whole tapestry of rules and values that would form the world of this Japanese version of chivalry—but the early tales of resilience and prowess became a foundation upon which all else could be built.

We have learned about all the different ways human resilience could manifest itself in the Japanese legendary world. From emperors to fishermen, from courage to kindness, we have seen varied depictions of heroism. We followed mortals who became deified and those who were entangled in the supernatural with varied consequences. In the upcoming stage of our journey, we will look more closely at these supernatural powers that often seek to meddle in our world. We will meet the *yōkai*, the spirits of the Japanese world, in all their mystery, wonder, and danger.

UNLOCK THE POWER OF SHARING KNOWLEDGE

"Stories hold the power to transport us to realms beyond our imagination."

— UNKNOWN

People who share stories selflessly open doors to new worlds and possibilities. So, if we have a chance to embark on such a journey together, I'm all in.

To make that journey possible, I have a question for you...

Would you share your experience with a book that has the potential to ignite curiosity and spark imagination in others?

Who are these individuals, you ask? They are like you—curious souls seeking to unravel the mysteries of the world around them, eager to dive into the depths of Japanese mythology.

My mission is to make the enchanting tales of Japanese Mythology accessible to all eager minds. Everything I do is rooted in that mission. And the only way for me to accomplish it is by reaching out to...well...everyone.

This is where your contribution matters. As they say, most people do judge a book by its cover (and its reviews). So here's my request on behalf of those curious minds you've yet to meet:

Please consider helping those explorers by leaving a review for this book.

Your gesture costs no more than a few moments of your time, but its impact could resonate with a fellow seeker for a lifetime. Your review could...

- ...guide another enthusiast to discover the wonders of Japanese Mythology.
- ...encourage a young reader to embrace their love for folklore and legends.
- ...inspire someone to delve deeper into the rich tapestry of culture.
- …guide a lost soul towards a newfound appreciation for ancient tales.

To experience that sense of fulfillment and truly make a difference, all you need to do is spare a moment to leave a review.

Simply scan the QR code below to share your thoughts:

If the idea of enriching the journey of a fellow explorer resonates with you, then you're already part of our community. Welcome aboard!

I'm thrilled to guide you through the captivating realm of Japanese Mythology, offering insights and tales that will broaden your horizons beyond measure.

Thank you from the depths of my heart. Now, let's dive back into the realm of legends and wonders.

- Your fellow explorer, Anthoney Poe

PS - Did you know? Sharing knowledge not only enriches others but also enhances your own value in their eyes. If you believe this book could light up someone else's journey, consider passing it along as a gift of inspiration.

3

YŌKAI —THE SUPERNATURAL CREATURES

At least once, every human has experienced that uneasy feeling that sometimes descends upon us at dusk. Shadows lengthen, and out of the corner of our eyes, we see unidentified shapes. Something seems to move in our peripheral vision, but nothing and no one is there when we turn around. Now, we tend to explain all our unusual experiences by tiredness or optical illusions. However, the Japanese tradition sees supernatural creatures in the shadows and mists, which was the case in the past and today. The yōkai wait for us behind every corner, telling an ages-old story about the truth of humanity: the need to describe and tame the unknown. Let's now take a deeper dive into the world of the Japanese supernatural, which will invite us to look beyond what can be seen with the naked eye.

THE ENIGMA OF YŌKAI

The word *yōkai* transcends the meaning of "monster" or "supernatural creature." It can refer to every phenomenon that is difficult to explain and can encompass monsters, apparitions, helpful spirits, and other creatures. The word itself can mean both "bewitching" (as in "attractive") and "suspicious" (Hirota, 2022; *Japanese Monsters*, 2019). Rather than associating themselves with more "official" versions of Shinto or Buddhist beliefs, the yōkai were, and still are, characters in folktales. Historically, the belief in various creatures varied considerably between cities and villages, and many local versions of the same creature would have different properties.

The belief in ghosts and monsters is known to humanity across cultures and ethnicities. Yet, the specific Japanese way has always been to ascribe nearly every sudden, or even everyday, yet unexplained phenomenon to a different creature. There are, in fact, hundreds of yōkai in various forms originating from different parts of Japan, and many of them have very narrow areas of interest. For instance, Zashiki Warashi specifically live in houses where they flip pillows and move furniture around when the inhabitants aren't looking. One type of yōkai would scare you at an empty crossroads, while another would haunt you on crowded streets.

Today, the yōkai penetrate Japanese pop culture and, as a result, have traveled beyond the borders of Japan. You can see them in mangas, games, and anime series. They constantly evolve and acquire new iterations. Let's now meet some of the most iconic examples of these mysterious creatures.

GALLERY OF THE SUPERNATURAL

Tengu

Red-faced and long-beaked, the Tengu look like demon-birds, both intimidating and grotesque. Often depicted in remote shrines, with their faces contorted by an upturned smile and with wings on their back, the Tengu are believed to be slightly dangerous. They live predominantly in the mountains and can kidnap unsuspecting people. Imagine walking alone in the woods and suddenly standing face-to-face with a haughty, humanoid goblin-bird!

The Tengu's character matches their looks. They are arrogant, to the point that they become a matter of proverbs. In Japan, if a person shows arrogance, their behavior could be likened to that of a Tengu. However, an unlikeable character is definitely the smallest of Tengu's vices. Their danger lies in the ability to disrupt public peace by their behavior, sometimes even by bringing about war.

The Tengu are powerful. They can be viewed as the yōkai but also worshipped like kami. Their origin story most likely lies within the Chinese culture, where they were portrayed as comets in the sky; their appearance was practically always a bad omen.

Some of the earliest stories involving the Tengu come from a collection called *Konjaku Monogatarishū* from around the 11th century. There, the creatures behave in all types of mischievous ways, robbing monks and kidnapping people. However, Japanese folklore also retained tales of how humans were able to trick the dangerous Tengu. One such person was Hikoichi, a young boy and a troublemaker.

Hikoichi lived in a mountainous village. It was believed that a Tengu resided on the outskirts of this settlement, and he had a magic cape that could turn its wearer invisible. When Hikoichi heard about that, he wished to possess that cape more than anything.

So, against all advice, he went out into the mountains, armed only with a bamboo stick. It wasn't long before a red-faced, long-nosed monster appeared before Hikoichi's very eyes, eager to spirit away a lonely traveler.

But Hikoichi stopped and, without warning, put his eye to his bamboo stick, looking through it like a telescope. This sparked the Tengu's interest.

"What do you have here?" the creature asked.

"It's a magic stick!" exclaimed Hikoichi. "You wouldn't believe the things it allows me to see!"

"Let me have a look," insisted the Tengu.

Hikoichi shook his head. "I wouldn't let you; you'd steal it."

It would have been easy for Hikoichi to request exchanging his stick for the Tengu's cape, but he was too clever for that. He knew that the creature might realize that the boy really wanted to obtain the cape. So, he waited patiently, feigning disinterest as the Tengu grew increasingly desperate to have the bamboo stick. Finally, the creature proposed the exchange himself.

Pretending to be reluctant, Hikoichi agreed. He handed the stick to the Tengu while the monster gave him the cape.

The Tengu looked through the stick, but he saw nothing extraordinary. Disappointed, he glanced up, ready to complain to Hikoichi, but the boy was already gone. He had put on the invisibility cape and ran away as fast as he could. And thus, he tricked a semi-divine monster.

Kappa

Kappa have undergone a series of transformations over the years. From a monster as dangerous, if not even more than the Tengu, it changed to an almost adorable creature reimagined in modern Japan as a mascot.

The Kappa is an aquatic creature. Its body is green and slimy, resembling the shape and stature of a child; however, it has webbed hands and feet, a turtle's shell on its back, and a bird-like beak. The top of its head is flat and circular, with scant hair growing around it. A small indent in the top allows the Kappa to accumulate water—its power source.

The Kappa's traditional activity was to lurk underneath the surface in lakes, pools, and streams and pull at the swimmers' legs, drowning them. Then, it would eat out their internal organs. Even more terrifyingly, the Kappa could sexually assault women and later force them to give birth to monstrous children.

Is it possible to escape the Kappa once it starts pulling at your legs as you swim? There are two ways of avoiding certain death: First, to lure it with a cucumber, a vegetable that the monster is particularly fond of. Alternatively, you could greet the Kappa in a Japanese fashion, with a bow. Since the creature, despite being dangerous, is very attached to rituals and politeness, it would feel obliged to respond with a bow. Then, the water accumulated on its head would flow down, weakening its powers. That is the moment when a victim could make their escape.

Over time, Kappa's slightly cartoonish appearance slowly caused the transformation of its nature—from dangerous to grotesque, then to somewhat ridiculous, then to cute. Today, Kappa can even appear in Japanese commercials and look almost like a human child if not for the flat circular top of the head and the turtle's shell.

The traditional association of Kappa with drowning is still preserved in some ways today: In public spaces in Japan, signs that forbid swimming in lakes or pools often use the image of a Kappa as a reminder.

Kitsune

Do you remember a little mysterious scene that I painted in the introduction to our tales? It is now time to get closer acquainted with the Kitsune, or the fox spirits.

It is important to note that the Japanese word *Kitsune* can mean both a regular fox and a shapeshifting one. It is perhaps unsurprising, as the Kitsune can be difficult to distinguish from ordinary animals—and, when they are in human form, from people. These creatures are characterized by an extremely long life (sometimes even reaching up to 1,000 years!) and superior intelligence. Their cunning often helps them trick humans, and they impersonate people of both genders—though more often, they show themselves as beautiful women. In this guise, they tend to seduce foolish men to get revenge for various offenses—most commonly, for taking away the land or livestock they wish to feast on. The Kitsune have a troubling ability to sense a person's greatest weaknesses—greed, pride, vanity—and take advantage of them for their own amusement.

The older the Kitsune, the more cunning they become. After the initial 100 years, they acquire the ability to shapeshift; however, they still retain some of their original fox-like features, which help distinguish them from ordinary humans. Narrow eyes and high cheekbones are the most prominent characteristics. However, the older the Kitsune get, the more they perfect their disguise. Instead of shapeshifting, some of them can also possess people, most commonly young women. Many urban legends exist in which an unsuspecting man married a woman possessed by a Kitsune, only to see his household ruined and his wife show demonic abilities. How does this manifest?

First, a Kitsune enters a woman's body through her fingertips or breasts. This would cause her to behave wildly and indecorously, such as running around naked, frothing at the mouth, or speaking in unknown tongues. All these are signs attributed to demonic possession across cultures, and it's not difficult to see this list of symptoms as a possible combination of a physical ailment and a mental illness. A woman possessed by a Kitsune can be exorcised at a shrine of the kami of foxes, Inari.

One can tell how old a Kitsune is by counting their tails. Typically, every 100 years means acquiring a new tail; some creatures possess as many as nine. After growing the ninth tail, a Kitsune changes its color from red to white or gold. Incidentally, cutting off Kitsune's tails can be the only way to kill them.

However, not all Kitsune are evil or mischievous. A separate category of good Kitsune exists who serve Inari and protect the gods' shrines. These benevolent foxes can be grouped under several categories. There are Kitsune associated with the elements:

Tengoku Kitsune, who only live in the sky and bring wisdom; Kaze Kitsune, who travel by wind at an extremely high speed; Kawa Kitsune, the reclusive water foxes; and Kasai Kitsune, the fire foxes. There are also other types, such as Seishin Kitsune, who transform themselves into humans to help rather than trick people. Lastly, Umi Kitsune are the oldest and most powerful kind, and they can be called upon for advice and healing. The god Inari can send all of these types of Kitsune as divine messengers to reward the deity's worshippers for their piety.

The benevolent Kitsune are associated with a beautiful yet tragic type of story. It is believed that many female Kitsune had fallen in love with human men and, in some cases, even married them. However, those unions almost always ended in tragedy or at least unhappiness.

In one of the stories, a Kitsune fell in love with a young man and transformed herself into a beautiful woman to marry him. The pair exchanged vows and lived together in marital bliss; soon, the fox-woman became pregnant. However, the husband was unaware of his wife's supernatural qualities.

That was also why he decided to acquire a dog—a natural enemy of a fox. On the day that the pair's baby was born, the man brought a little pup into the house. The fox-woman grew frightened and unhappy, but she didn't dare to speak up for fear of being exposed and her beloved husband casting her away from the house.

Unfortunately, the strife between the wife and the dog continued as the animal grew larger and would frighten the fox-woman with its barking. One day, it startled her so much that her magical powers broke, and she turned into a wild fox.

When the husband returned home, he heard the cries of his baby. His wife was nowhere to be found, but he spotted a glimpse of a fox in their garden. The mystery was resolved at night when the fox-woman suddenly came into the house again and, in tears, confessed everything. She could now no longer retain her human form during the day, but she could come back every night to lay with her husband. The man forgave the deception, and the marital life resumed, albeit with some degree of separation. This tale could have ended much more tragically. In many stories, the fox-wife has to escape from the neighborhood, fearing the wrath of her neighbors.

This story doesn't specify what happened to the couple's child, but over the ages, many people in Japan have been suspected to be the descendants of Kitsune. Such people would always be believed to possess supernatural powers that they could pass on to the next generations.

As we can see, the Kitsune can contain multitudes of personalities and stories; one should be prudent to know both how to repel and attract them. Remembering to cut off the additional tails and leaving out fried tofu for the benevolent Kitsune is perhaps the safest way to interact with these supernatural creatures while in Japan.

Jorōgumo

Slightly more terrifying in appearance than the Kitsune—at least to some part of the population—Jorōgumo is a giant spider with shapeshifting abilities. Deceptively, this spider can change into an enchanting young woman. However, she often retained her eight spindly legs growing out of her back. It is believed that every spider can turn into a Jorōgumo as long as it lives for 400 years.

Then, it grows in stature, up to two meters high, and finds its lair in remote corners of forests.

Rather than tricking and humiliating humans as the mischievous Kitsune do, the Jorōgumo have a much more nefarious agenda—they aim to devour their victims whole. As beautiful women, they would often course the streets at night in search of overly excitable men, then promise them a time full of pleasure. When the victim agrees, they would take him to a remote location and, while drawing him near, entangle him in their web. The man would watch in horror, helpless and bound, as the woman's beautiful face merges with her neck, her body changes into a round corpus, and her back grows eight legs. Nobody would hear the victim's cries for help.

However, there are some would-be victims of the Jorōgumo who had survived. One man from Izu passed by a beautiful waterfall after a full day of work and decided to nap. When he awoke, he found himself entangled in a web. Still tired, he brushed the web off his clothes and wiped his hands on a nearby bush. Fortunately for him, the web hadn't been built strong enough yet when he awoke.

He fell asleep again, and when he next woke up, the bush next to him was torn to pieces. Alarmed, the man jumped to his feet and ran away. He realized that he had almost been killed by a Jorōgumo.

This man's story ended well for him only because it lacked the element of seduction. Every tale that begins with a young man falling in love—or at least in lust—with a Jorōgumo ends with a man's death, usually in a rather gruesome way.

Tsuchigumo

Another spider-like creature, the Tsuchigumo, is not only a deceiver but also a straight-up predator. These giant, monstrous spiders are said to live underground in caves and caverns. Because of this behavior, they are often associated with rebels. Some legendary accounts about the early Japanese emperors mention the rulers subduing some Tsuchigumo, which could be read both as a mythological tale of fighting with monsters and a more historical account of fighting dissidents. Emperor Jimmu himself is believed to have subdued a Tsuchigumo and then cut its body into several pieces and scattered them in different locations—thus preventing the spider from regenerating.

As monsters, the Tsuchigumo have goblin-like faces attached to their large bodies, which can contain multiple human victims. In one adventurous story involving Minamoto no Yorimitsu, a late 10th-century general, Yorimitsu encountered a giant Tsuchigumo in a remote mountain cave.

The general had been gravely ill with malaria. One day, as he lay bedridden and suffering from delirious visions, a monk suddenly appeared by his bedside. He looked like an ordinary person, but there was something off in his stature. Initially, Yorimitsu took him for another delusion—but then, suddenly, the monk loomed over the sick general and attempted to capture him.

Despite his illness, Yorimitsu reached for his side and caught his sword, a famous katana named Hizamaru. He slashed at the monk's robes, leaving a gash across his stomach. The stranger recoiled and ran away, leaving a bloody trail behind him.

Even though Yorimitsu was still gravely weakened from his sickness, he took his sword and servants and followed the predatory monk. The journey took them to a nearby mound, where they found a cave with a giant, over-one-meter-high spider. After a valiant fight, the general opened the spider's stomach with his katana. Imagine his surprise when immediately, almost 2,000 heads of Tsuchigumo's victims rolled out! Additionally, some skulls and smaller spiders were found in the monster's stomach.

Now, miraculously, the malaria left Yorimitsu's body, and he realized that the illness had been the Tsuchigumo's way of trying to weaken him. Claiming victory, The general displayed the spider's corpse for all to see and renamed his sword Kumo-kiri, the "Spider Slicer."

Zashiki Warashi

We are returning from the realm of murderous monsters to much more hospitable and cozy households, where Zashiki Warashi, mischievous house spirits, tend to have fun by playing minor pranks on people. Making strange noises, leaving footprints all over the house, or slightly moving the furniture seem to be their primary areas of interest. Most of the time, Zashiki Warashi are invisible. However, on the rare occasion they show themselves, they look like semi-transparent ghosts of a blushing child. Despite their slightly rude behavior, the Zashiki Warashi are believed to guard households and protect their inhabitants from sickness. Even more than that, they can also become companions and keep loneliness at bay. They befriend and play with children and take care of elderly and infertile couples.

It is no wonder that the presence of Zashiki Warashi in one's home is highly desirable. People would go to many lengths to lure these spirits to their doorstep. Leaving out food and burying a golden coin in the house's foundations seems to be the most efficient way to do so.

With such a friendly countenance, Zashiki Warashi easily found their way to modern Japanese entertainment. There are even types of Pokémon based on them. The children-like ghosts populate mangas and anime series and even appear in literature. However, amidst all the cuteness and playfulness, it is often forgotten that the ghostly children share a chilling origin story. In the older times, when plagues and famines were no strangers to Japanese lands, the Zashiki Warashi were believed to have been the spirits of children who died during such disasters. In some even more gruesome versions of the story, the Zashiki Warashi had originally been children who had been killed by their own parents. These were often extremely brutal and tragic tales of parents who, in poverty, could not support their children and resorted to desperate means. Nowadays, however, this sad tale is mostly forgotten, and the Zashiki Warashi remain friendly household spirits.

Tanuki

The Tanuki, similar to the Kitsune in their shapeshifting abilities and the love of mischief, are nonetheless less intelligent and far less dangerous than the malicious brand of magical foxes. The Tanuki are raccoon dogs who love playing tricks on humans but are also signs of good luck.

In their proper form, the Tanuki resemble the Japanese raccoon dogs, minus their large bellies, which can play like a drum, and the hats they wear. They can also fount to carry a multitude of items, among them a bottle full of sake and bags with gold. Thus depicted, a statue of a Tanuki symbolizes good luck, kindness, and openness of heart. It's a trendy addition to a Japanese home, either as a little figurine or a stuffed animal.

The Tanuki can change their shape into humans but more often into inanimate objects. Today, it is mostly believed that they use these powers for mischief or to be helpful to humans who were kind to them. However, some older tales preserved an image of a much more nefarious Tanuki. One of these tales is called *Kachi-Kachi Yama*, and the Tanuki is definitely a villain in this story.

The story goes as follows: An old couple lived together in a village house. However, they were troubled as a mischievous Tanuki kept wreaking havoc in their fields. One day, the old man managed to capture the creature. He tied it up and brought it to the house, intending to kill it and cook it for dinner. Then, he went out again to work in the fields.

The man's wife saw the Tanuki miserably wailing in the corner. Initially, she didn't pay it any mind and started preparing some mochi, a sweet rice dish. But the cries were getting louder and louder, and the woman turned to the Tanuki, irritated.

"I can help you make the dish," Tanuki offered, "If you set me free."

The woman shook her head. She didn't want to relent, as she feared a trick, but the creature's cries were getting unbearable. Finally, she agreed to free the Tanuki.

This was a tragic mistake. The malicious creature jumped on the poor woman and killed her. Then, it chopped her body into pieces and, using its shapeshifting powers, turned into the dead woman.

That was when the old man came back home. He entered the house to the smell of a delicious soup being cooked by his wife. Gladly, he sat down at the dinner table and ate the dish. He barely managed to finish it when suddenly, something horrible happened: His wife dropped her spoon and started shifting. Soon, the Tanuki stood before the man, clapping its paws in cruel glee.

The man paled. "What did you do to my wife?" he asked.

The Tanuki laughed coldly. "Why, you have just eaten her! Have you not noticed her bones that I hid under the floorboards?"

With that, the Tanuki ran away, leaving the poor man in shock and disgust.

This was too big of a crime to be overlooked. Fortunately, the old man had a good friend: a talking rabbit. The animal promised that he would avenge the old woman's death. Simply hurting the Tanuki would be too good for it; the malicious creature had to taste betrayal. So, the rabbit approached the Tanuki and pretended to befriend it. Only when the Tanuki started trusting and inviting him to be its company did the rabbit put his plan into motion.

He would pretend to injure the Tanuki by accident. When the creature complained about the pain, he would rub a salve mixed with pepper into its wounds, making them sting much worse. But the greatest pain came when the rabbit had sneakily set the Tanuki's fur on fire.

The Tanuki walked a couple of steps, feeling slightly off. It heard the sound of a fire crackling and smelled smoke. The sound of the fire resembled the words *kachi-kachi yama*—hence, the tale's title. Soon, the Tanuki was crying out in pain, badly burned, though not dead.

At that moment, the Tanuki realized that the rabbit had been a false friend. The creature challenged the animal to a swimming contest: They were each to build a boat and swim through a lake, and the one to drown would lose both the contest and their life. The rabbit agreed, but to ensure his victory, he secretly altered the build of his and the Tanuki's boats. They both looked the same, but where the rabbit's boat was built out of a tree trunk, the one belonging to the Tanuki had been secretly constructed out of mud.

It was no wonder that the next day, while in the middle of the lake, the Tanuki's boat started dissolving. The victorious rabbit swam closer and started poking at the creature with his oar, trying to sink it even faster.

"Why have you betrayed me?" cried the Tanuki.

"You don't know it yet?" the rabbit responded. "It is revenge for what you did to the poor old woman and her husband. I have long been their friend."

With that, he pushed the Tanuki underneath the surface. The creature died with the knowledge of its own malice being its undoing. Finally, the rabbit would return to the old man's house and relay the whole story to him, giving him solace in knowing that the woman's life had been avenged.

I do not wish to leave you with this gruesome story as the only representation of a Tanuki's behavior. In many other tales, these creatures are quite helpful. The most famous one, *Bunbuku Chagama*, tells the story of a particularly funny and kind Tanuki.

The title word *chagama* refers to a particular Japanese tea kettle. In our tale, a monk was the owner of this object. When he put it over a fireplace, the kettle suddenly started moving. Growing paws and a tail, It had been a disguised Tanuki all along. Seeing that he would have no use of the kettle, the monk sold it to a traveling merchant.

It wasn't long before the merchant discovered that he had been gifted with a Tanuki. He wanted to eliminate the creature, but it begged him to save its life. It then jumped onto a tightrope stretching over the top of the merchant's cart and started performing acrobatic tricks.

"You can show me around as an attraction," the Tanuki said. "I will perform these tricks if you treat me well."

The merchant agreed. From then on, he started touring the entire country, showing off his magical kettle, coming to life, and dancing on a tightrope. Soon, people began flocking around to see the performance, and the man became rich.

Today, the character of a Tanuki appears everywhere. It is shown in highly popular video games such as *Super Mario Bros 3*, where Mario can wear a Tanuki suit, allowing him to fly and turn into a statue (*Japanese Raccoon Dog*, n.d.). It also appears in *Naruto* and *One Piece*. As a figurine, they can be found at every corner and have become emblematic of Japan.

Oni

We have already met Oni, the goblin-like demons Momotaro defeated. Of course, the Oni stronghold our hero had destroyed was by far not the only place they could be found. They are believed to inhabit numerous locations across Japan. They would often behave aggressively, taking over villages and shrines and creating their encampments there.

It is within the Oni's nature to be greedy, evil, and selfish. In a way, they are the embodiments of the worst vices that can be found within humanity. There exist many types of Oni, and some of them include Gaki, ever-hungry Oni who personify gluttony; Kijo, the female Oni who kidnap children and raise them to become evil; Ushi-Oni who impersonate cows and eat people in the fields; Zenko, murderous Oni who inhabit graveyards; and Terai Oni, who live in forests and hoard treasure and can also change their gender.

Throwing soybeans at them is the most common way of driving the Oni away. Leaving a trail of beans around one's house is an especially effective tactic. Paradoxically, dressing up in an Oni costume might also repel the real Oni and drive away bad luck. For this reason, Japanese men would often wear demon masks in colors varying from red to green or blue and participate in parades.

Apart from the story of Momotaro, there are also a couple of other tales featuring the Oni. In most of them, they are firmly villains, but one tale is starkly different from the others—a sad and touching one.

There once lived a pair of Oni friends, one blue and the other red. Despite his fearful appearance, the red Oni was not your typical monster: He wished to become friends with the humans. However, whenever he approached human settlements, the people would run away from him in fear.

This made the red Oni cry. When his friend, the blue Oni, saw what was happening, he devised a plan to help his friend. He would mock-attack the nearby villages, giving the red Oni the opportunity to save the people from his attacks.

The plan worked. Soon, the people would witness a fearsome blue Oni attacking their settlements, only to then notice a red Oni fight off the attacker and save the people. Soon, the red Oni acquired a reputation for being helpful.

Seeing this, the blue Oni was content. He had helped his friend. But he also knew he couldn't be seen in the company of the red Oni anymore since it would cause the people's suspicion to rise. So, he left his friend and retreated into the wilderness.

When the red Oni discovered his friend was gone, he understood his sacrifice. He cried for a second time: He had gained new friends in the form of humans but had lost an old companion.

Kuchisake-Onna

The story of Kuchisake-onna is tragic and terrifying. She used to be a mortal woman, a beautiful wife of a very powerful samurai. Sadly, her husband was hardly at home, always spending his time at war. Kuchisake-onna grew lonely and sought the company of other men. From a playful conversation to a stolen glance, the woman started having an affair.

People in her town talked, and it wasn't long before the news of the betrayal came to the samurai's ears. Furious, he returned home, and upon seeing his wife, he slashed the corners of her mouth with his knife, creating the ghastly, bloody, Joker-style smile. Other versions of this legend are even more gruesome. They claim that to make sure his wife would never betray him again, the samurai ordered a dentist to replace her teeth with sharp fangs, which then sliced her mouth open.

After her death, Kuchisake-onna became a vengeful ghost. She roamed the streets of cities at night, knife in hand, her face covered with a mask. She would approach young men and ask them only one question: "Do you think I am pretty?"

There is no correct answer to this inquiry. If the victim said no, Kuchisake-onna would reach for her knife and plunge it into the unfortunate man's heart. If, however, the victim responded with a yes, she would take off her mask to reveal her mutilated face. "Even now?" she would ask again.

The sudden revelation of Kuchisake-onna's bloody face could cause a person to scream or change their answer to a no. Then, they, too, would be killed by her knife. If, however, the victim answered yes, she would spare their life but, in turn, slice their mouth open the same as had been done to her.

So, is there any way of escaping Kuchisake-onna once she already asked her question? The short answer is: A victim must keep the ghastly woman distracted. They may refuse to play her game by not responding to the question and instead hurrying along. They might throw candles or money at her to divert her attention. Or, they might respond to her question: "Your beauty is average," and while Kuchisake-onna ponders on how she should react to that response, the victim can run away.

With such a tragic backstory and murderous tendencies, it is no wonder that Kuchisake-onna became a popular character in the more horror-aligned works of modern Japanese culture. A 2007 horror film called *Carved: The Slit-Mouthed Woman*, as well as its sequels, explored the legend (Fordy, 2019).

Kuchisake-onna closes our gallery of the Japanese supernatural. We have met creatures both terrifying and funny, dangerous and helpful. We have seen how some of the yōkai could be both at once. This duplicity conveys an important truth about the human response to their existence within the universe. Everything unknown, understudied, and wild can be conceptualized in the monstrous face of a powerful creature. Still, on the other hand, everything familiar, such as foxes or raccoons, can also have a more uncanny side. The Japanese people repeatedly prove how they notice the supernatural within the ordinary. The yōkai's nature is ever-mysterious and elusive. Yet, their existence helps better explain the universe's unpredictable nature.

Japanese mythology comes in cycles of perpetual change and renewal. We have seen how some of the yōkai transformed from dangerous creatures to funny tricksters, changing their properties and functions over time. In the next stage of our journey, we will look at this tendency to change within the context of a bigger picture: myths of creation and destruction. Get ready for this next step, as it will take us back on a trip through the far corners of the universe.

4

MYTHS OF CREATION, DESTRUCTION, AND RENEWAL

W e are now returning to the larger picture of the Japanese universe—but this time, we aim to examine how the vision of the creation and possible future destruction of the world leaves a mark on society. The Japanese myths reflect some larger truths about the cyclical character of nature and individual life— and that finds its way into the organization of private and public life, as conceptualized in Shintoism and the Japanese version of Buddhism. To note how this manifests, we will revisit the creation story and how the world of Kami intersects with that of people. We will also examine the Japanese visions of the end of the world and how the fear accompanying them manifests throughout beliefs and customs. Lastly, we will see how these tales influenced Japan in the past, leaving their mark on an agrarian society that revolved around the everlasting cycle of changing seasons.

THE ORIGINS

Remind yourself of the dark and chaotic beginnings of the universe in Japanese mythology. Remember the chaos and the floating particles that slowly formed the High Heavenly Plain, the Earth, and the underworld. Look again at Izanagi and Izanami using their spear to order the earthly particles and create the first Japanese island. In Shintoism, the gods are the ones to bring order into the universe; it is no wonder that they first emerged when the chaos spontaneously started ordering itself.

Apart from ordering, the gods also had the power to create, whether new hosts of gods or natural phenomena; the line between the two is somewhat blurry, as we have already witnessed. In the Japanese language, a particular word is used for the ability to create or for the ability to possess a life force —*musubi*. Possessing musubi means being able to give birth to powerful beings to form a chain of creation, reaching from the highest beings to the lowest, as exemplified in the narrative about people being the descendants of the gods.

Because of the gods' world-ordering qualities, the best way of life for humans was to follow them. The name of the original Japanese religion, *Shinto*, literally means "The way of the gods." Following and appeasing the kami was a challenging task. As we have seen, the gods can be both benevolent and wrathful. For that reason, many customs were developed within Shintoism, with ritual purification at their core. Spiritually motivated cleanliness was a necessary step before entering any shrine through the *torii* (the T-shaped gates). Failure to follow this rule might result in a disaster, whether on an individual or a societal scale.

The ancient Japanese prayed for luck and prosperity, but they also feared destruction. Most likely, that misfortune would come in the shape of a war, a plague, or a famine... But what would happen if it were more total? In short, how did the Japanese envision a possible end of the entire world?

WHEN WORLDS END

As we have seen, the legend of Amaterasu hiding in the cave and depriving the world of sunlight is a core myth in the Japanese tradition. This story, framed as a tale of anger and jealousy, was also a fearsome tale of a possible biological disaster. The ending of the tale, with the god of wisdom Omoikane sealing the entrance to the cave and ensuring that Amaterasu would never hide herself again, was supposed to be a reassurance. The sun would never again hide; the cosmic order was restored. Still, a faint echo of fear remained—that the nation that prides itself on living in the Land of the Rising Sun might one day wake up to eternal darkness.

Another fear of destruction is highly connected to Japan's geographical location, with its recurring earthquakes. No matter how terrifying, the monsters and yōkai of the Japanese bestiary are overshadowed by Namazu, a giant catfish believed to live deep in the ocean whose stirring body causes disturbances.

However, in true Japanese fashion, a story of chaos and destruction must be resolved with at least a small semblance of order. It was believed that once upon a time, Namazu's movements were so wild and uncontrolled that the earthquakes wrecked Japan even more than they do today. The gods needed to rectify this situation, so they sent a god of thunder, Takemikazuchi, on a mission to subdue the giant catfish. Takemikazuchi had been one of the gods who emerged when Izanagi, blinded by grief, cut the body of the fire god Kagutsuchi into pieces. This kami possessed a heavy magic rock that he used to weigh down Namazu's head, restricting its movements and thus lowering the frequency of the earthquakes it caused. This rock was so enormous that its bottom rested firmly on Namazu's head, but its tip still protruded from the Earth's surface. It is believed that the tip of this rock can still be seen today in the Kashima Shrine near Tokyo—one of the most important shrines in Japan. The stone looks like a rather unassuming rock. Still, according to the legend, any attempts at excavating it failed, as the workers couldn't find the rock's bottom even after several days of digging.

Namazu exemplifies the Japanese belief in the balance between the forces of chaos and order. Even though destructive, the fish's behavior can also be a means of just punishment and retribution. During the 19th century, a belief arose that claimed Namazu's earthquakes were a way of enacting a cyclical renewal of nature and society through destruction. This idea, called the *yonaoshi*, spoke primarily to the lower classes that believed Namazu was, in a way, an avenger and an agent of retribution, acting on their behalf and disrupting the stiff and unjust social order. Symbolically, the giant catfish represented a chance for the poor to inherit the rich's wealth and gain individual good luck.

It is undoubtedly fascinating to see how the two ideas present in Japanese society—that of the importance of order and the creative power of destruction—coexisted and interacted throughout history. Some disasters are justly feared, but sometimes, an end might also mean a new beginning.

THE CYCLES OF SEASONS AND LIFE

The cyclical nature of the changing seasons, individual life, and the broader scheme of destruction and renewal is a recurring theme throughout many stories and beliefs in Japanese mythology. The society we today associate with modernity and rapidly advancing technology for ages was predominantly agrarian. It is no wonder that numerous religious practices and beliefs are tied to this highly cyclical way of life.

Tanokami and His Festivals

One way in which these practices would manifest was the beliefs grouped around Tanokami, the god of rice fields and harvests. This god has multiple iterations depending on a region, and many festivals and observances are tied to his person. The god doesn't have a single official depiction. In some areas, he is represented by a stone statue; in others, bundles of branches are believed to be his symbol. Scarecrows would also be often deified as representations of the god.

The statues of Tanokami can be periodically decorated with cherry blossoms or painted in bright colors during celebrations dedicated to him. During spring and autumn especially, that is, at the time of rice planting and harvesting, the number of these festivals rises.

The first festival of the spring is called Minakuchi-matsuri. It is a ritual greeting of Tanokami, with various rituals surrounding it. Some of them may include putting decorative wands containing cherry blossoms and roasted rice up in the fields where the new rice of that year will be planted.

Upon the planting of rice, farmers practice *Saori*—the ritual greeting of Tanokami in the rice fields. At the end of planting, *sanaburi* is performed to send Tanokami off the fields. Farmers would bring young rice plants home and dedicate them to their household kami.

The rice planting itself is a significant event. This practice, often called *otaue*, would usually be performed by female planters (*saotome*). Viewed as more than simply field workers, these women would be referred to as servants of the gods. On the day of planting, they would wear their best clothes and would often sing as they performed their duty, accompanied by Japanese flutes, drums, and bells. The food eaten on the day of planting is considered sacred and is ritually shared with Tanokami.

After the planting and growing of rice, there comes the time of reaping. During the day of Hokake, newly harvested rice ears are brought home and offered to the gods. Later, at the end of September, the festival of Kariage or Mikunichi is held at the end of harvest, depending on the region. During Kariage, rice ears are gathered and piled up in the form of an idol, which is then worshipped like the god Tanokami. In other regions that celebrate Mikunichi, rice balls are covered with red beans and offered to Tanokami.

In October, a couple of other harvest celebrations are held. Mochi rice cakes are most often offered by children at household shrines during the festival of Tokanya. At Inoko, kids eat rice cakes and walk around with sticks, beating the ground in a symbolic act of soothing the Earth after it has given the people its fruits.

New Year Celebrations

Several other deities connected to the cyclical passage of time and everyday life permeate the Japanese common consciousness. Another god of harvest is Toshigami. His connection to the cycle of reaping and sowing over time morphed into an association with time itself. As a result, he became a titular deity of a starting new year.

The traditional Japanese New Year celebrations are connected to the Lunar New Year; however, since the late 19th century, they have been moved to January 1. This celebration for Toshigami is closely tied to the harvest. During that day, at family gatherings, people would give thanks for the last harvest and pray for an upcoming year of bounty. Houses would be decorated with pine branches, which are supposed to serve as a guiding sign for Toshigami; the god would only visit a decorated home. Sharing and offering specific food is also essential during the New Year: Rice cakes offered to Toshigami would later be submerged in *ozoni*, a miso-based soup.

Sorei-Shin and Yashiki-Gami

Just as there are specific Shinto deities responsible for guarding time, there are also gods who take care of space—specifically, domestic space.

The Yashiki-gami are domestic deities who take care of individual houses and families. They most often have a shrine within the house and are believed to dwell either within a garden or an enclosure adjacent to the building or in a nearby forest. At least some of these gods are the spirits of the ancestors, Sorei-shin. Their area of patronage also encompasses agriculture, embodying an important lesson: One is tied to one's land through the spirits of people who came before. An individual's connection to their ancestors creates a link between the mortals and the gods, blurring the lines between the ordinary and the supernatural.

Kitsune-Zuka

Do you remember the benevolent fox spirits who serve the god of foxes, Inari? This all-encompassing deity presides over many aspects of life, and one of them is also connected to agriculture and rice. One of the myths connected to a female element of Inari (who can be portrayed both as a man and a woman) exemplifies that.

It was said that when the Earth was first formed, it was still disorganized and had yet to separate entirely from the surrounding water. As a result, the land was swampy, and it lacked proper grain that could be cultivated there. It was no wonder famine soon struck the Earth, and the early people were dying in dozens.

That was when Inari descended from the High Heavenly Plain, riding a white Tengoku Kitsune, bearing heaps of grain in her hands. This was *ine*, which would later become the word to denote rice. From that point onward, famine was much easier to avoid. To celebrate Inari's helpful role in humanity, the deity is often depicted with a bag of rice, which signifies plenty and prosperity. Before currency became widespread in Japan, people would often use rice as a form of payment—and so, when money replaced food, Inari became a patron of prosperity in any form.

Other Agricultural Deities

Agriculture truly was the backbone of ancient Japanese society—and so, Shintoism revered many more deities connected to agriculture and food than the ones we have already discussed. Let's meet these fascinating kami.

Ogetsuhime, or Ukemochi, and Tsukuyomi

Let's now briefly come back to the sad tale of how the moon god, Tsukuyomi, killed Ukemochi for her lack of manners and was, for that reason, shunned by Amaterasu. Ukemochi—or Ogetsuhime—is, of course, an important goddess of food. Despite her early death, she is credited with vital aid to humanity. After her death, a manner of foodstuffs grew out of her corpse. Silkworms crawled out of her head, rice and millet grew out of her eyes and ears, her nose produced red beans, and wheat and soybeans grew out of her private parts. This seemingly gross and gruesome process brought abundance to all humanity.

Because of his unfortunate encounter with Ukemochi, Tsukuyomi became associated with agriculture. His identification as the moon especially served this purpose, as the Japanese traditionally used the lunar calendar to set the rhythm of the yearly agrarian cycle.

Okuninushi, Onamuchi, and Omononushi

Okuninushi, also known as Omononushi, is an essential god. A descendant of Susanoo, he was for a time the lord of the Central Land of Reed Plains—the Earth, which he inherited from his noble ancestor. Okuninushi was the first to turn the Japanese islands from wet marshland into firmer ground.

Okuninushi is a kind god whose behavior serves as an example of how nature should be treated. The god displayed these characteristics from an early age. The youngest of many siblings, he was always much gentler than his brothers. Back then, he was known by the name of Onamuchi.

One day, exciting news circulated the land: Princess Yagamihime of Inaba was looking for a husband. Instantly, Onamuchi's brothers jumped at the opportunity. They decided to travel to Inaba together. When Onamuchi learned about this, he approached his brothers.

"Let me go with you," he pleaded.

The brothers laughed. Onamuchi was not only the youngest but was also the weakest one of them.

"We will allow you to travel with us," the brother said, "But only if you act as our bag carrier."

Not minding the humiliation, Onamuchi agreed. Soon, the brothers set out on a journey. They traveled with pomp and splendor while Onamuchi trotted behind them, panting and sweating under the combined weight of their luggage.

As the brothers were riding down the road, they spotted a curious sight: a skinned rabbit was writhing on the side of the road. The poor creature was in agony from its wounds and called out for help. The brothers' hearts were cruel. They advised the rabbit to wash in salt water and dry its wounds in the wind afterward. Then, laughing, they rode away.

Unsurprisingly, when the rabbit followed the advice, its agony only grew. It wept and cried even more than before. That is how Onamuchi, who had been lagging behind the group, found the poor creature.

Pity instantly overtook the young boy. He put down his bags, helped the rabbit bathe in fresh water, and then instructed it to roll around in pollen. Instantly, the animal's wounds healed themselves.

Princess Yagamihime had many spies in her land. She soon found out about the whole incident and condemned Onamuchi's brothers' cruelty. Only Onamuchi himself was worthy of her hand. By showing how to care for the tormented rabbit, he set an example of how everyone should treat nature around them.

Unsurprisingly, Onamuchi's brothers didn't like this turn of events. Onamuchi would never be allowed to spend time with his new wife. His brothers conspired to kill the young god by devising a number of impossible challenges that they then compelled him to complete. First, they ordered him to catch a red wild boar. Onamuchi didn't know that the supposed animal was, in fact, a boulder heated up to redness and rolled down a mountainside. He grabbed the rock, and it burned his skin away from his body. Onamuchi died on the spot.

However, the mother of the god was not having this. She took the rainbow bridge to the High Heavenly Plain and begged the gods to restore life to Onamuchi. Remembering Onamuchi's previous kindness, the gods agreed and reincarnated him as a young man, even more handsome than before.

That was when Onamuchi's brothers tricked him for the second time. They trapped him in a tree log, where he died of hunger and thirst. And yet, Onamuchi's mother pleaded for his life again—and again, new life was granted.

Onamuchi knew that his brothers would not rest until they killed him, but he also didn't wish to test the gods' patience for the third time. He escaped from his ancestral land and lived in exile in the land of Ki.

Upon seeing Onamuchi, the wise elders of Ki told the young man that he had a destiny to fulfill. It was his task to finally defeat his brothers and become the sole ruler of Earth. To achieve that goal, he had to seek out his noble yet wild ancestor, Susanoo. The god of wind now lived in the underworld.

Onamuchi set out for a dangerous journey. He descended into the underworld through a hidden passage. The darkness of the place intimidated him; he only vaguely remembered the two previous times when he was dead and had to descend into the underground palaces—but the experience sent shivers down his spine.

His fear subsided, however, when upon reaching Susanoo's hidden palace, Onamuchi was greeted by the most beautiful woman he had ever seen. This was Suseribime, Susanoo's daughter. Onamuchi instantly fell in love with her, and she reciprocated his feelings.

But Susanoo wasn't happy with this. Being of a disruptive nature, he was very protective of his daughter. Devising several traps, he intended to end Onamuchi's life.

Seemingly unperturbed, Susanoo invited Onamuchi to his palace and put him in a bed chamber. That room, however, was full of venomous snakes crawling over the floor and walls. Fortunately, Suseribime, suspecting her father, lent Onamuchi her magical scarf. Once the hero wrapped himself in it, it protected him from the snakes.

Susanoo was far from done with testing the hero, however. He transferred Onamuchi to another room, this time full of centipedes. Suseribime's scarf protected the young man again, so Susanoo had to devise a different tactic.

The wind god shot an arrow far into the fields and commanded Onamuchi to fetch it. As the young man labored through the fields, Susanoo set the entire field on fire. That was the right moment for Onamuchi's love of the Earth and its creatures to turn into an advantage: As he was choking on the smoke, a little mouse spotted him and took pity on him. It showed Onamuchi a hidden way out of the fields. When the fire subsided, the hero found Susanoo's arrow and returned it to him.

Susanoo felt defeated but still hesitated to give Suseribime away to Onamuchi. He decided he rather liked the young boy as his slave, and he gave him a gross order: to pick out lice from his hair.

Onamuchi set to work. While performing the long and arduous task, he massaged some red clay into Susanoo's temple. This clay had been another gift from Suseribime, which lulled her father to sleep. Once the wind god was deep in slumber, Onamuchi tied his hair to the rafters of his house, took Suseribime's hand, and fled as fast as he could. Before he did, though, he also stole Susanoo's bow, arrows, and a stringed instrument named *koto*.

Onamuchi's recklessness almost proved his undoing. As he was escaping the underworld, the koto slipped out of his bag and brushed against a nearby tree, giving out a racket. This woke Susanoo.

The wind god groaned, realizing what had happened. He jumped to his feet and ran after Onamuchi and Suseribime, pursuing the pair deep into the land. But Onamuchi was faster. At last, Susanoo was forced to relent. He gave Onamuchi his blessing and renamed him Okuninushi-no-Kami ("Master of the Great Land"). In addition, Suseribime was given the name of Utsushikunitama-no-Kami ("Spirit of the Living Land").

Now, newly fortified by his adventure and Susanoo's weapons, Okuninushi could finally challenge his brothers. He defeated them easily, and the whole Earth was now his. He could organize the Central Land of Reed Plains in a way that made life for humans more bearable.

Okuninuchi's story repeats a motif that we have already seen in the tale of Urashima Taro: Kindness to nature and its creatures is a highly praised trait in Japanese society. Okuninushi, as the master of the Earth, also exemplifies some of the cyclical features of nature: His double death resembles the death of plants in winter, and his resurrection imitates the yearly onset of spring.

Toyokanome, or Toyokehime

No traditional Japanese meal would be complete without a drink. Just as rice and other foods have deities traditionally ascribed to them, so does *sake*, the Japanese alcohol.

Toyokanome, also known as Toyokehime, is the goddess of sake. The legend connected to her had her as one of the beautiful goddesses living in the High Heavenly Plain, who one day put on a robe made of feathers and descended on the Earth to bathe. As it happened, an old childless couple overlooked the goddess' descent and stole her robe as she was bathing. Without the garment, Toyokanome couldn't return to heaven and remained on Earth, becoming the couple's adopted daughter and sake brewer. After the pair's death, Toyokanome started brewing sake for all humanity. Thus, alcohol became quite literally a heavenly drink brought down to the Earth.

The gods and stories we recounted in this chapter are an obvious example of how deeply the cycles in nature impacted Japanese society. The patterns of death and renewal found their reflection in stories and worship. Many recurring themes are visible throughout, including a need to treat nature with kindness and dignity, respect for the food that sustains us, and gratitude for those who can provide it. As we have seen, these values and patterns are visible not only in tales but also in the annual cultural practices of the Japanese people. In the next stage of our journey, we will learn more about rituals and celebrations—from individual practices to communal activities. We will see what makes the Japanese culture and way of life so unique.

5

RITUALS, FESTIVALS, AND CULTURAL PRACTICES

I invite you to step again under the bright orange torii gates leading to a Shinto shrine—this time, at sunrise. You will walk a path of purification as the first sun rays shine through the gates, reflecting off the wood in a way that seems to light it on fire. As you approach the shrine, you see the sloping wooden roofs and hear the deep calls of the bells. The sun rises from behind the structure as if the goddess Amaterasu herself slept inside the sacred place. You feel a sense of timelessness as you see the shrine bathed in light. Below, bustling life reminds you of modernity and day-to-day rush, but here, you realize that some things never change. For centuries, the Japanese have worshipped the kami in their annual rituals and consecrated shrines. For ages, these customs stayed unchanged. Now, I invite you to delve into this world of exuberant festivals and sacred rituals that color the seasons, relate to the past, and celebrate the continuum of life.

THE SACRED THREAD OF SHINTO RITUALS

Shinto is unlike most religions we know. It doesn't have sacred texts or a list of faith tenets; there are no obligatory services to attend. Priests can be male or female, although a male priest is often aided by a female attendant who also communes with the kami in a shamanistic way. In fact, Shinto is such a decentralized religion that possibly the only common element its rituals and practices possess is the worship of the Japanese kami. Maintaining harmony between the world of the gods and the people is Shinto's primary objective.

Not having an obligatory service doesn't mean the believers never frequent the shrines. Some people visit them daily; others choose the first and 15th days of each month. Yet others visit the rituals only on the days of unique festivals called the *matsuri*. None of these ways of worship is considered better or worse than others.

Ritual purification lies at the heart of Shinto worship. It is, however, essential to understand that this purification is not the means of repelling evil from a person's heart. Its purpose is to keep evil spirits at bay. In Shinto, evilness is believed to come from the outside, not from within.

In a way, coming to a Shinto shrine is like visiting an important person in your life. The sacred places are believed to be, quite literally, homes of the kami. In that case, what etiquette should be followed at a shrine?

Most practices in Japan's sacred places are optional; however, there are two main rules to follow: keeping quiet and purifying ourselves with water before entering to rid ourselves of any possible evil spirits. There are a couple of possible methods of purification: *haraigushi* or *ohnusa*, that is, touching a special wand that is supposed to absorb a person's impurity and later destroy it;

or *misogi harai*, or submerging oneself under natural running water (such as a waterfall), the way that Izanagi once did after fleeing from Yomi. In addition to these practices, purification can also be performed on a larger scale. Each year, after June and December, mass purification is performed in the shrines across Japan, aiming to purify the entire population.

Other practices performed within Shinto shrines include ritual dances and prayers. The dances are a reminder of when Amaterasu hid herself in the cave, and the gods had to appease her by entering a religious frenzy. Prayers, on the other hand, have many forms. They can follow a complicated structure, including praising the kami, listing one's offerings, and enumerating requests. The offerings can include special wooden plaques called *ema*. The visitors to the shrines don't only have to give, however; worshippers can receive amulets of good luck with the kami's names inscribed on them; alternatively, for a much cheaper price, a slip of paper with a fortune written on it.

Apart from the public festivals (matsuri), the life of a Shinto believer consists of many private celebrations, marking important stages in one's life, such as birth, entering adulthood, getting married, or building a house. From 30 to 100 days after a child's birth, they are brought to a shrine dedicated to their tutelary kami and initiated into the religion. Similarly, marriage vows also take place before the kami. Simply put, any major milestone in one's life can be celebrated with the presence of the Shinto gods.

However, an important distinction is made for funerals. Since death is considered impure in Shinto, funeral rites are delegated to Buddhist shrines and monks. There would be a period of time when a believer wouldn't enter a Shinto shrine after having experienced the death of someone close to them for the reason of impurity.

Shinto rituals evolved over time. After Buddhism was introduced to Japan in the sixth century C.E., the initial conflict period slowly led to peaceful coexistence and the reinterpretation of Buddhist doctrines in the Shinto style. For example, some prominent Buddhist figures were incorporated into Shinto as new kami, and the kami themselves started to be regarded as the incarnations of Buddha. However, the coexistence of Buddhism and Shinto was forcibly severed in the 19th century, when attempts to preserve Japanese national identity caused Shinto to be installed as a state religion. This ended in the 20th century, however. Shinto priests are no longer state officials, and the worship is much more personalized.

Now that we know the basics about Shinto rituals, it is worth mentioning which shrines are the most important to the religion— and also most worthy of a visit while on a trip to Japan.

Fushimi Inari Shrine

The row of vermilion torii gates I urged you to imagine in the introduction to this book is perhaps one of the most iconic sights associated with Shinto shrines in Japan. It is also located at the Fushimi Inari Shrine in southern Kyoto. The number of gates outside of the shrine reaches thousands; all of them are dedicated to the shrine by a different business venture, and all bare, beautifully painted, and inscribed. The shrine itself is dedicated to the kami of foxes Inari, and you can see countless fox figures and images when you visit.

Ise Grand Shrine

Perhaps the most significant shrine in all of Japan, the Ise Grand Shrine (located in Ise near Nagoya) is dedicated to the goddess Amaterasu and is believed to have been erected by Princess Yamatohime, the aunt of Yamato Takeru, over 2,000 years ago.

However, don't look for ancient structures when you visit the site. It is believed in Shinto that the shrine has to be torn down and rebuilt every 20 years. This fascinating approach signifies Shinto's cyclical approach to life and nature.

Apart from its ancient history, the shrine is also connected to one of the most sacred objects in Japanese myth. The Eight-Span Mirror, the one that, according to the legend, was used to lure Amaterasu out of her cave, is believed to be held in the shrine.

Ise Grand Shrine is a large complex. It consists of over 125 buildings. Every year, over 6 million people visit the site.

Itsukushima Shrine

Itsukushima Shrine is located on Miyajima Island in Hiroshima Bay. It was constructed partly on a floodplain and is known for its iconic large "floating" torii gate that is submerged in water during high tide. The unique design of the shrine is a result of the belief that erecting the building on firm land would offend the kami of the island.

Apart from the gate, the shrine is also adjacent to a theatre building dating to 1590. It has been a scene in many *noh* plays— classic Japanese dramas. The theatre was also constructed over the water.

Itsukushima Shrine is a UNESCO World Heritage Site and one of the must-see locations in Japan.

Toshogu Shrine

Extravagantly colorful, Toshogu Shrine is nested in the mountains near the town of Nikko. Red and gold are major color schemes in this intricate building, and ornate wooden carvings covered with gold leaf would dazzle any visitor. Toshogu Shrine is also an unusual Shinto site: It contains the remains of shogun Tokugawa Ieyasu (1543–1616), which is almost unheard of given Shinto's position on impurity surrounding death.

Izumo Taisha

Izumo Taisha shrine in the city of Izumo might be the oldest Shinto shrine in Japan, although its exact age is unknown. Okuninushi, the Lord of the Land of the Reed Plains, is the titular kami of the temple. It is believed that around November, he hosts all the other kami of Japan for a meeting at the shrine.

The shrine is primarily known for its large central hall. Married couples often visit this site, as Okuninushi is believed to also be the kami of marriage. As a form of purification, visitors would customarily clap four times before entering the site, twice for themselves and twice for their partners.

Meiji Jingu Shrine

Compared to other Japanese shrines, the Meiji Jingu Shrine is relatively new. It was completed in 1920 and is dedicated to Emperor Meiji and his wife, Empress Shoken—agents of the Meiji Restoration, which saw Japan's westernization and rapid technological advancement. The shrine was destroyed during World War II but was later rebuilt and is a top-rated tourist destination today.

Tsubaki Grand Shrine

If you live in the United States and wish to get a taste of Japanese shrines but lack the means to travel to Japan, the Tsubaki Grand Shrine awaits you. Constructed in 1987 in Granite Falls, Washington, it is the only public Shinto shrine in the mainland United States. One of the kami venerated there is Ame-no-Uzume, the goddess who lured Amaterasu from her cave with her dance.

Yasukuni Shrine

The Yasukuni Shrine in Tokyo is a controversial site but definitely a must-see if you are an enthusiast of recent history. It was first erected by Emperor Meiji in 1869 and dedicated to the spirits of those who died in the service of the Emperor: men, women, children, and even animals. However, as a result of the recent turbulent Japanese history, over 1,000 individuals enshrined there are considered war criminals who committed horrible crimes against humanity. To this day, the museum affiliated with the shrine has been stating highly controversial opinions about Japan's involvement in World War II.

Sengen Jinja Shrine

Located at the base of the famous Mount Fuji, the Sengen Jinja Shrine is home to an 18-meter-tall torii gate. As we saw with the story of the fire god Kagutsuchi, whose mutilated body transformed into volcanoes, the worship of mountains, and especially volcanoes, as gods lies at the heart of Shinto beliefs.

Sanno Shrine

Lastly, the Sanno Shrine is another chilling memory of Japan's recent history. The shrine has survived the bombing of Nagasaki—despite being located only 800 meters from the epicenter of the explosion!—and consists of only half of a torii gate. For this reason, it is known as the "one-legged shrine," a moving symbol of endurance.

THE CALENDAR OF JOY: ANNUAL FESTIVALS

In Japanese, *matsuri* is best translated as *festival*. Japan has countless such festivals since every shrine celebrates one of its own. Originally instated to commemorate a particular kami of the shrine, over time, the matsuri became more connected to changing seasons or local traditions, not necessarily religious in nature. Dances and processions with miniature portable shrines (*mikoshi*) are an essential part of most matsuri.

Festivals largely vary by region. However, there are a couple of celebrations common to the entirety of Japan.

Obon

Obon, or Bon Matsuri, is a festival celebrating the ancestors and the spirits of the dead. Its development is a result of merging the Shinto belief in one's ancestors becoming the kami and the Buddhist practices surrounding the dead, which were influenced by Chinese culture and its Ghost Festival. The celebration is held in July or August, depending on the region, and lasts approximately three days.

The most crucial feature of Obon is the dance called Bon Odori. It is an old folk tradition, reaching back almost 600 years. Various regions would practice unique dance moves and play diverse music during the ceremony. However, the most common form of dance throughout Japan is for a group of dancers to form a circle around a wooden stand called a *yagura*.

Bon Odori is not only a festive dance. Its moves have a symbolic meaning and refer to the history of the region where it is performed and the prominent people who passed away. In short, the dance is an artistic expression of regional identity and a history lesson.

The most famous regional variation of Obon is the Awa Odori Festival in Tokushima, which is celebrated in mid-August. The Bon Odori dance is believed to have originated there. During the festival, the dancers are divided into teams that compete with each other, often dancing for hours on end.

Tanabata

Tanabata, or the Star Festival in July or August, is a festivity celebrating the stars Vega and Altair. A tragic story is connected to the kami of these stars. Princess Orihime, a living star and a daughter of the king of the sky, Tentei, was a heavenly weaver and produced a beautiful tapestry known as the Milky Way. However, despite her stunning work, she was unhappy, as the weaving took all of her spare time. She worried that she would never be able to meet anyone and fall in love.

Seeing his daughter's sadness, Tentei arranged a meeting for her. He called a kami of another star, a young boy named Hikoboshi. He was a celestial cowman, herding stars in the sky like one would herd cows.

When Hikoboshi and Orihime saw each other, they instantly fell madly in love. They both forgot all about their duties. Orihime no longer weaved the Milky Way, and Hikoboshi's stars started dispersing in the sky, leaderless. Tentei saw this, and his concern grew. In the end, he felt like he had no choice: He had to separate the two lovers, placing them on the opposing sides of the sky.

Orihime wept, heartbroken. She begged her father to reconsider, and when he refused, she asked him to at least let her meet Hikoboshi once a year. Tentei reluctantly agreed. Furthermore, the two lovers were allowed to meet on the seventh day of the seventh lunar month.

When the day came, Orihime gladly ran in Hikoboshi's direction. The pair stopped, however, each standing on the opposite side of the celestial river Amanogawa. The river's current was too strong; they couldn't cross. Orihime wept again, and her cries were so loud and desperate that a flock of magpies came and spread their wings, creating a bridge upon which Orihime could cross the river and embrace her lover.

In some years, the river would be even more unpredictable, and the magpies would be unable to help. For that reason, it is said that if the day of Tanabata is rainy, Orihime and Hikoboshi have to wait until another year—and the rain is referred to as their tears.

Traditional celebrations of Tanabata vary across Japan, but most commonly, boys and girls make their wishes on that day. Girls wish for better craftsmanship, especially weaving, and boys for better writing skills. The wishes would be written down on colorful strips of paper and hung from tree branches, especially that of bamboo.

One especially famous regional variation of the Tanabata is celebrated in Sendai on August 6–8. During that time, the entire city is covered with giant, dazzling, colorful decorations, fireworks shows, and musical performances.

Local Festivals

Nagasaki Lantern Festival (Late January/Early February)

The Nagasaki Lantern Festival is the first significant festival of the Japanese year. As the name suggests, the celebration's main attraction is the myriad lanterns produced and lit up against the dark winter sky. The festival's origin lies in Chinese culture, in the Lunar New Year celebrations. Today, the epicenter of the festivities takes place in the Chinatown district of Nagasaki, and it is a sight to behold. The dazzling play of light attracts over a million spectators every year.

Sapporo Snow Festival (Late January/Early February)

A celebration of winter in all its icy glory, the main attractions of the Sapporo Snow Festival are the large snow and ice sculptures. The festival proves how Japanese culture has evolved and enriched over time. The celebration isn't ancient and, instead, started in 1950 when a group of local students built a couple of snow figures in a park. Today, the constructions made out of snow are much more elaborate and feature exact replicas of famous buildings worldwide. Typically, over 100 sculptures are created every year.

Hakata Dontaku Matsuri (May 3–4, Fukuoka)

In late April and early May, Japan enjoys a holiday period called the Golden Week. The Hakata Dontaku Festival in Fukuoka is one of the most iconic staples of that time. It has been celebrated for over 800 years and features two grand parades with dancers wearing traditional costumes and colorful floats. On the evening of each celebratory day, the spectators are encouraged to join in the dances.

Kanda Matsuri (May, Tokyo)

Held in the Kanda Myojin Shrine in Tokyo, the Kanda Festival is one of the largest celebrations in Japan's capital. The origins of the festivity lie, yet again, with the famous shogun Tokugawa Ieyasu and his victory over the army of Western Japan in the Battle of Sekigahara in 1600. It was believed that the shogun's visit to the Kanda Myojin Shrine before the battle ensured his victory.

Today, however, this militaristic origin is all but forgotten, and the festival's primary purpose is to wish for general prosperity and good luck. The main feature of the celebration is a grand parade through four districts of Tokyo: Kanda, Nihonbashi, Otemachi, and Marunouchi.

Tenjin Matsuri (Late June–July 25, Osaka)

Osaka is known as the unofficial second capital of Japan, and the Tenjin Festival does justice to this title. A very ancient practice spanning over 1,000 years, it celebrates the kami of scholarship, Sugawara Michizane, also known as Tenjin.

The festival features a procession on boats on the Okawa River. Men dressed in colorful costumes and beating drums are an iconic sight during this time. The month-long celebrations are concluded with a lavish display of fireworks, which is an unforgettable experience for anyone visiting Japan in the summer.

Gion Matsuri (July, Kyoto)

The Gion Festival in Kyoto proudly claims the title of the oldest in Japan: It originated in 867 C.E., when a plague ravaged Japan. The first festival was held to assuage the kami and drive away the sickness.

Today, the festival lasts for a whole month. On the 17th and 24th of July, two major processions with 29 floats take place. All of the floats are considered treasures of the Japanese culture. During the processions, the participants and spectators alike dress in traditional kimonos. For a moment, anyone who sees the celebrations can be transported to Japan from long ago.

Kishiwada Danjiri Matsuri (Mid-September)

The yearly festival in Kishiwada near Osaka has one distinct feature: The floats pulled during the traditional parade are made out of wood, making them one of the heaviest existing in Japan—up to 4 tons! Watching these constructions being transported through Kishiwada is to admire the extraordinary strength of those responsible for this monumental task.

Aomori Nebuta Matsuri (Early August)

The Nebuta Festival in the Aomori Prefecture is known for one of the most iconic floats. Each of the illuminated paper constructions features a famous warrior or a group of warriors, their original purpose being symbolic representations of the dead who would be sent away into the spirit world during the festival.

Each warrior float is surrounded by groups of dancers wearing traditional costumes called *haneto*. Throughout the city, stands are put up with haneto costumes ready to buy; once you wear this traditional garb, you are allowed to join the dancers in their festive performance.

The Nebuta Festival closes our overview of Japanese matsuri. As we have seen, these celebrations can encompass all areas of life, from preventing disease and religious celebrations to displaying arts and crafts or simply having fun. The Japanese festivals are all about celebrating beauty in all its forms.

As you have also undoubtedly noticed, some of the matsuri originated outside of Japan, mainly from China. Throughout the ages, the seemingly remote island archipelago fell under the influence of various cultures. In the next chapter, we will learn more about how Japan incorporated foreign elements into its myth and culture. We will also trace some common aspects of Japanese myths found in other worldwide mythologies. Get ready for this extraordinary journey through the universal human experience.

6

INFLUENCE AND RELATIONSHIP TO OTHER CULTURES

A wave never truly belongs to one place. It travels on the sea, reaching faraway lands. Water can carry objects to distant locations overnight, but aren't words a bit like waves? Over the centuries, Japanese stories of gods, heroes, and spirits have traveled, transformed, and returned enriched by varying elements of other cultures. In the last stage of our journey, you will learn the tale of cultural exchange—not only of direct influences but also of shared human heritage.

NEIGHBORING SHORES: CHINESE AND KOREAN INFLUENCES

It is probably unsurprising that the civilizations positioned geographically closest to Japan—those of China and Korea—also left the most significant imprint on Japanese myth and culture. The cultural exchanges between the three countries span over hundreds, if not thousands of years. They are both tales of peaceful inspiration and influence dictated by militaristic aggression. The relations between China and Japan are more a tale of an older civilization (China) teaching its ways to the younger one (Japan). On the other hand, the relations between Japan and Korea have always had a bit more of an equal standing to them, even though they weren't always peaceful—as we saw with the story of Empress Jingu and the supernatural conquest of Korea.

China

Buddhism came to Japan from China, and so did the art of rice cultivation, the first form of writing, the style of clothing and architecture, and much, much more. The first trade relations between China and Japan go back to the year 400 B.C.E. (Cartwright, 2017). At that time, ancient China had already gone through three imperial dynasties. It was a firmly established power in East Asia, while Japan was only at the cusp of finding its identity. Hence, Chinese influences on the Japanese mythical landscape are profound and far-reaching.

Let's explore some examples of similarities between Chinese and Japanese myths, as they start in the very beginning, with the primordial chaos before the creation of the world. According to the Chinese, this chaos was also the primal state of existence; however, the Chinese creation myth emphasizes the elements of yin and yang. These active and passive particles separated from each other, creating the world. The concepts of yin and yang and the philosophy surrounding them are firmly Chinese ideas, slightly less present in Japanese culture. However, the echoes can still be heard throughout its creation story.

Since Chinese Buddhism traveled to Japan, so did the figures and Chinese gods associated with this faith. In Japan, they transformed into kami. There are many examples of such influence, but one of the most famous includes a group known as the Seven Lucky Gods —seven Japanese deities who are believed to bring prosperity and fortune. Apart from the already-known and purely Japanese Ebisu, all the other gods in that group are of Chinese origin. Additionally, many Japanese kami connected to the stars originated in China since the knowledge of astronomy and astrology was another aspect of Chinese culture that traveled over the sea to Japan through Korea. The story of the stars Orihime and Hikoboshi and their accompanying festival of Tanabata originated in China.

On the topic of festivals, many matsuri are also of Chinese origins. The Nagasaki Lantern Festival is, of course, the starkest example. In general, the celebrations of the Chinese New Year are very popular in Japan.

Not only the gods but also the monsters found their way from China to Japan. The line between the two is thin in both cultures. Take the Chinese dragons, whose wisdom places them among the gods. The figure of a dragon is a prominent feature in Japanese myths. It is not only a vicious beast to be eradicated, like in the story of Susanoo killing Orochi, but also a powerful kami that can guard various natural phenomena. The beautiful daughter of the sea, Otohime, who was so grateful for Urashima Taro's help, was, in fact, a daughter of the Dragon King of the ocean.

Many other yōkai are of Chinese origin. One example is Kirin, a chimeric animal, a combination of a dragon, a horse, and a deer. In China, this creature is called the Qilin. It is believed to be an omen appearing when the ruler of the land is especially virtuous and distinguished.

Despite the numerous influences and similarities, Japanese mythology is still clearly distinct

from China's. Its unique features are known throughout this book's pages, from Shinto and its kami to the cyclical approach to time and nature.

Korea

We have witnessed the fascinating yet highly militaristic narrative about Empress Jingu conquering two Korean kingdoms, Silla and Paekche. This tale was used in the 20th century by the expansionist Japanese government to justify not only the conquest of Korea but also the most brutal war crimes committed against the Korean people. If we look further in time, we will see that the story of terrible wounds had not always been the truth of relations between Korea and Japan.

In fact, many ancient Chinese ideas and inventions traveled to Japan through Korea. Between the sixth and eighth century C.E., the culture of the Paekche kingdom helped spread the teachings of the Chinese philosopher Confucius and the Chinese writing system. It is known that during that time, Korean scholars and artists traveled to Japan and were welcomed at the Yamato court. Sometimes, various Korean kingdoms would be at war, and refugees from these wars would flee to Japan.

As a result, both Korea and Japan were influenced by the Chinese culture, and both also exchanged ideas and stories between themselves. In fact, it is sometimes difficult to establish the exact origin of certain elements of Japanese culture: Did it travel directly from China, influencing Korea independently, or was Korea the midway stop? In some cases, it is impossible to know.

One important and interesting feature of both Korean and Japanese beliefs is the shamanic nature of some of the rituals. We have seen shamanism feature prominently in the tale of Empress Jingu. Such practice is also present in the Korean tradition in the form of the folk religion of Muism. These shamanistic practices may have traveled from Korea to Japan when the narratives of the first Japanese emperors were constructed and influenced some motifs in these tales.

SIMILARITIES WITH OTHER MYTHS

Across cultures worldwide, myths bear similarities to each other—even if the two cultures in question never had the opportunity to interact or even know of each other's existence. This, of course, is at least partly a result of a shared human experience: We all sleep at night and labor during the day. We experience natural disasters and seasonal changes, even in different climate zones. We associate the sun with warmth and power and cold with death and food deprivation. We all have mothers, fathers, grandparents, siblings, cousins...

Sometimes, the similarities can be eerily surprising. Other times, historians and anthropologists can trace a faint thread of influence where it was not previously expected. This will be the case in some of the elements of Japanese myth that I am about to compare to stories from civilizations far, far away.

Greek

Let's start with the most surprising example. Do you remember Fujin, the demon of wind who chased Izanagi out of Yomi? He is most commonly depicted as carrying a windbag containing typhoons. This depiction, however, is common to the Japanese kami. It can be traced back to the Chinese god of wind, Fengbo. But Fengbo and his depiction were influenced by the Pakistani civilization of Gandhara—which, in turn, was influenced by Greek art and the depiction of a Greek god of wind, Boreas. What an extraordinary journey! It was only made possible thanks to the existence of the Silk Road—the pan-Asian trade route that transported goods and ideas from Southern and Eastern Europe, through the Middle East and India, to China and beyond.

The similarities between Greek and Japanese myths don't end at that fascinating tidbit. Suppose you are in any way familiar with Greek mythology. You might associate the phrase "In the beginning, there was chaos" with the Greek creation story. Although the Greek Chaos can be personified as a god, whereas the Japanese primordial state of disarray is entirely faceless, the similarity is right there.

Izanagi's journey to Yomi in search of his dead wife Izanami also resembles the classic Greek story of Orpheus and Eurydice. Orpheus's love for his wife moved him to try and change the laws of the universe by venturing into Hades and taking Eurydice back to earth. Orpheus's plan almost succeeded—he would have managed to revitalize his wife if he hadn't turned to look at her in the last moment of his journey, overcome by doubt. That broke a rule imposed on Orpheus by Hades and caused Eurydice's spirit to disappear from before her husband's eyes.

In contrast, when he sought out Izanami, Izanagi was met with a more gruesome image of death. There was no bargain with any underworld lord, only the sad fact of death. But it is still an interesting parallel—how the hero's journey into the land of the dead ends in failure because he dares to look at his beloved, expecting to find the same woman he grew to love when she was still alive.

Indian

If you were to look for similarities between Japanese and Indian myth and folklore, you would find more than you think. The simplest reason for this is the indirect influence of Indian tradition on Japan: Buddhism first traveled from India to China and was then absorbed by the Japanese. As a result, many kami I mentioned before were directly borrowed from China and can eventually be traced back to India. Three of the Seven Lucky Gods —Daikokuten, Bishamonten, and Benzaiten—have their Indian equivalents in Mayahana Buddhism or Hinduism: Mahākāla, Vaiśravana, and Saraswati, respectively. Dozens of other Japanese kami also have their Indian equivalents.

Additionally, there are some similarities between Shinto and Hinduism, possibly stemming from indirect influence and similar experiences in the surrounding world. In Hinduism, humans are believed to ultimately be descendants of the sun, which resembles the great reverence the Japanese give Amaterasu. The approach to the harmony between humans and the world surrounding them is also similar.

Celtic

An interesting case is to be made between various Celtic traditions (including Irish and Welsh) and some themes in Japanese mythology. In the tragic story of Urashima Taro, the fisherman spent three days in the ocean kingdom, which equaled 300 years on Earth. This type of story, where the hero is transported into some kind of fantastical "other-world," features prominently in Irish folktales. The belief in the Fairy Kingdom, or the alternative reality of Tír na nÓg, usually entails a story of a human snatched away by elves—either in a forest or while traveling to fantastical lands. The human hero would spend a couple of days with the elves. Still, upon his return to the mortal lands, he would discover that hundreds of years have passed and nobody recognizes him any longer. This is a fascinating parallel between two cultures from opposite sides of the world.

Similarly, a parallel can be drawn between a famous hero from Wales and the Japanese legendary warrior Yamato Takeru. When Western anthropologists first started studying Japanese mythology, the story of Takeru reminded them a lot of King Arthur. Both heroes are given magical swords that legitimize their authority, both are leaders of warrior bands, and both lose their power when they foolishly leave their swords behind in the care of a female companion.

All the similarities and influences that we have traced in the last stage of our journey emphasize the universal nature of Japanese myth while also paying attention to its uniqueness. The stories we have told in this book are ancient, and so were the exchanges with other cultures; however, today, the culture of Japan continues to engage in dialogue with the rest of the world. Through reworkings of old heroes and creatures in modern pop culture, Japan exports the best characters from its stories globally and, in turn, draws inspiration from abroad, both from other Asian countries and from the West. In the age of globalization, cultural exchange happens at an accelerated speed—but Japan retains the unique character of its myth.

KEEPING THE ADVENTURE ALIVE

Now that you've journeyed through the depths of Japanese Mythology with us, equipped with newfound wisdom and insights, it's time to pay it forward and keep the spirit of exploration alive.

By sharing your genuine thoughts about this enchanting voyage on Amazon, you're not just reviewing a book; you're igniting the curiosity of other young adventurers, guiding them to embark on their own odyssey through the wonders of Japanese Mythology.

Your review is more than just words; it's a beacon illuminating the path for fellow seekers of knowledge. Together, we can ensure that the tales of ancient gods and heroes continue to captivate hearts and minds for generations to come.

Thank you for your contribution in preserving the legacy of Japanese Mythology. Every review is a testament to the enduring power of storytelling and the boundless realms of imagination.

Simply scan the QR code to share your thoughts:

Let's keep the adventure alive, one review at a time.

CONCLUSION

Our journey through the enchanting realm of Japanese myths, legends, and rituals has been nothing short of extraordinary. From the primordial darkness that birthed the universe to the emergence of gods and heroes, we've traversed epochs of time and layers of existence, immersing ourselves in the vibrant tapestry of Japanese culture.

Throughout our odyssey, we've borne witness to pivotal moments in Japanese mythology: the wrenching grief of Izanagi as he bid farewell to his beloved wife, the triumphant exploits of Momotaro as he vanquished the fearsome Oni, and the bittersweet tale of Urashima Taro, caught in a timeless dance with the mysteries of the sea.

Our journey has been colored by encounters with a diverse cast of characters—from the eerie allure of the Jorōgumo to the mischievous antics of the Tanuki—each embodying facets of human emotion and experience that resonate across cultures and generations.

But our exploration extends beyond mere storytelling. We've traversed the sacred precincts of ancient shrines, where the echoes of prayers mingle with the whisper of the wind, and we've reveled in the kaleidoscopic splendor of traditional festivals, where the spirit of community thrives amid the dance of lanterns and the rhythm of drums.

Yet, as captivating as our journey has been, it is but a prologue to a larger narrative—a prelude to the countless tales and traditions that lie in wait, eager to be unearthed and shared. I implore you to continue this quest, to delve deeper into the depths of Japanese folklore and unlock the mysteries that await discovery.

Embrace the parallels we've drawn between Japanese mythology and other cultural traditions, and let them serve as springboards for your own creative endeavors. Whether through storytelling, artwork, or scholarly inquiry, your contributions have the power to enrich our understanding of these timeless tales and forge connections that transcend borders and boundaries.

As you embark on this continued journey, may the radiant light of Amaterasu illuminate your path, guiding you through realms of wonder and enlightenment. May the stories shared within these pages continue to inspire and captivate audiences for generations to come, ensuring that the legacy of Japanese mythology endures for all time.

REFERENCES

5 important Shinto shrines in Japan you need to visit. (n.d.). JRPass. https://www. jrpass.com/blog/5-important-shinto-shrines-in-japan-you-need-to-visit

Abbas, L. O. (2023). *Are the creation stories of ancient Japan and ancient Greece more similar than we expect?* Classics for All. https://classicsforall.org.uk/rostra/are-creation-stories-ancient-japan-and-ancient-greece-more-similar-we-expect

The accomplished and lucky tea-kettle. (n.d.). Sur La Lune Fairytales. https://www. surlalunefairytales.com/books/japan/freemanmitford/ accomplishedteakettle.html

All about Kitsune. (2018, April 3). WAttention. https://wattention.com/mythical-creature-kitsune/

All you need to know about the ancient Japanese gods and goddesses. (2023, May 27). Old World Gods. https://oldworldgods.com/japanese

Amaterasu. (2019). Encyclopedia Britannica. https://www.britannica.com/ topic/Amaterasu

Annual events and folklore customs in Japan. (n.d.). Tokyo Restaurants Guide. Retrieved January 25, 2024, from https://restaurants-guide.tokyo/column/ annual-events-and-folklore-customs-in-japan-part-1

Ashkenazi, M. (2008). *Handbook of Japanese mythology.* Oxford University Press.

Aston, W. G., & Chamberlain, B. H. (2005). *The Kojiki: Records of ancient matters.* Tuttle.

Averbuch, I. (1998). Shamanic dance in Japan: The choreography of possession in Kagura performance. *Asian Folklore Studies, 57*(2), 293. https://doi.org/10.2307/ 1178756

Bathgate, M. (2004). *The fox's craft in Japanese religion and culture.* Routledge.

Boardman, J. (2023). *The diffusion of classical art in Antiquity.* Princeton University Press.

Bon Odori. (n.d.). Japan hoppers—Free Japan travel guide. https://web.archive.org/ web/20200727012627/https://www.japanhoppers.com/en/all_about_japan/ culture/214

Borsotti, M. (n.d.). *People from Japanese lore: Yamato Takeru.* Wasshoi Magazine. https://www.wasshoimagazine.org/blog/discovering-japan/yamato-takeru

Brians, P. (2016, November 14). *Japanese creation myth (712 CE).* WSU. https:// brians.wsu.edu/2016/11/14/japanese-creation-myth-712-ce

Bushido. (n.d.). New World Encyclopedia. https://www.newworldencyclopedia. org/entry/bushido

Cartwright, M. (2017, June 27). *Ancient Japanese & Chinese relations*. World History Encyclopedia. https://www.worldhistory.org/article/1085/ancient-japanese--chinese-relations

Cartwright, M. (2016, November 25). *Ancient Korean & Japanese relations*. World History Encyclopedia. https://www.worldhistory.org/article/982/ancient-korean--japanese-relations

Cartwright, M. (2012, December 6). *Izanami and Izanagi*. World History Encyclopedia. https://www.worldhistory.org/Izanami_and_Izanagi

Cartwright, M. (2017). *Namazu*. World History Encyclopedia. https://www.world history.org/Namazu

Cartwright, M. (2012, December 19). *Susanoo*. World History Encyclopedia. https://www.worldhistory.org/Susanoo

Cartwright, M. (2017, May 15). *Yomi*. World History Encyclopedia. https://www. worldhistory.org/Yomi

Chart, D. (2021). *Takamagahara or Takamanohara?* Mimusubi. https://www. mimusubi.com/2021/10/12/takamagahara-or-takamanohara

Chiba, R. (1995). *The seven lucky gods of Japan*. Charles E. Tuttle.

Chinese mythology vs Japanese mythology: A comparative exploration of ancient Eastern legends. (2023, November 13). Old World Gods. https://oldworldgods.com/chinese/chinese-mythology-vs-japanese-mythology

Comparing Japanese & Chinese cultures: Similarities and differences. (2017, February 6). Experts Column. https://travelandculture.expertscolumn.com/comparing-japanese-chinese-cultures

Csorgo, S. (2017). *10 popular Japanese festivals*. Tsunagujapan.com. https://www. tsunagujapan.com/10-popular-japanese-festivals

Daisaburō, H. (2014, April 3). *Kami: The evolution of Japan's native gods*. Nippon. https://www.nippon.com/en/in-depth/a02902/

DeMarco, M. (2016). *Women and Asian martial traditions*. Via Media Publishing.

Dyer, H. (2014). *Japan in world politics, a study in international dynamics—primary source edition*. Nabu Press.

Emperor, imperial rescript denying his divinity (professing his humanity). (2019). National Diet Library. https://www.ndl.go.jp/constitution/e/shiryo/03/056shoshi.html

The farmer and the badger. (n.d.). Wikisource. https://en.wikisource.org/wiki/The_ Japanese_Fairy_Book/The_Farmer_and_the_Badger

Ferber, C. (n.d.). *O-Kuni-Nushi-no-Kami; Prince Ruddy Plenty*. Japanese Buddhist Statuary. https://www.onmarkproductions.com/html/O-Kuni-Nushi-no-Kami.html

Fordy, T. (2019, March 7). *Sadako lives: The true stories behind five Japanese horror movies.* The Telegraph. https://www.telegraph.co.uk/films/0/ring-grudge-japanese-horror-movies-true-stories

Foster, M. D. (n.d.). *Yōkai: Fantastic creatures of Japanese folklore.* Japan Society. https://aboutjapan.japansociety.org/yokai-fantastic-creatures-of-japanese-folklore#sthash.o4qwANIa.R1CnZuDQ.dpbs

García, H. (2010). *A geek in Japan: Discovering the land of manga, anime, Zen and the tea ceremony.* Tuttle Pub.

A guide to Japanese monsters: Tanuki. (2021, November 14). Bokksu. https://www.bokksu.com/blogs/news/a-guide-to-japanese-monsters-tanuki

Greenberg, M. (2020, December 21). *Tsukuyomi the moon god: The modern guide.* Mythology Source. https://mythologysource.com/tsukuyomi-japanese-god

Hannah, D. (2019, August 6). *24 temples & Shinto shrines to visit in Japan.* All Japan Tours. https://alljapantours.com/japan/culture/history/religion-and-spirituality-sites-in-japan

Hearn, L. (1988). *Glimpses of unfamiliar Japan: In two volumes.* Rinsen Book.

Hearn, L. (2015). *The romance of the Milky Way and other studies & stories.* Read Books Ltd.

Heaven, hell and reeds: Japanese myths. (2020, September 30). Sunway Echo Media. https://sunwayechomedia.com/2020/09/heaven-hell-and-reeds-japanese-myths/

Hirafuji, K. (2019). *Yamato Takeru: The hero who pacified the East with the sword Kusanagi.* Kokugakuin Media. https://www.kokugakuin.ac.jp/en/article/130837

Hirai, N. (2019). Shintō—ritual practices and institutions. In *Encyclopædia Britannica.* https://www.britannica.com/topic/Shinto/Ritual-practices-and-institutions

Hiroshi, I. (n.d.). *Daikokuten.* Encyclopedia of Shinto. https://d-museum.kokugakuin.ac.jp/eos/detail/?id=9943

Hiroshi, I. (n.d.). *Tanokami.* Encyclopedia of Shinto. https://d-museum.kokugakuin.ac.jp/eos/detail/id=9973

Hirota, R. (2022). Traversing the natural, supernatural, and paranormal: Yōkai in postwar Japan. *Japanese Journal of Religious Studies, 48*(2), 321–339. https://doi.org/10.18874/jjrs.48.2.2021.321-339

Imada, K. (2023, February 2). *9 most beautiful traditional festivals in Japan.* Time Out Tokyo. https://www.timeout.com/tokyo/things-to-do/the-most-beautiful-traditional-festivals-in-japan

Interesting comparison of Japanese and Korean mythology. (2005). All Empires. http://www.allempires.com/allempires.com-redirect/forum/forum_posts.asp?TID=1837

Izanagi and Izanami. (2020). In *Encyclopædia Britannica.* https://www.britannica.com/topic/Izanagi

Japanese festivals (matsuri). (2019, May 24). Japan Guide. https://www.japan-guide.com/e/e2063.html

Japanese festivals: What is a matsuri? (2020, April 11). SNG. https://www.sng.ac.jp/en/sng-news/japanese-festivals-matsuri/

Japanese folklore and mythology. (2019). New World Encyclopedia. https://www.newworldencyclopedia.org/entry/Japanese_folklore_and_mythology

Japanese kami of food and agriculture. (n.d.). Japanese Buddhist Statuary. https://www.onmarkproductions.com/html/food-kami.html

Japanese monsters, ghosts, and spirits: Mythical Yōkai (妖怪) at OSU libraries. (2019). Osu.edu. https://library.osu.edu/site/japanese/2019/09/09/japanese-monsters-ghosts-and-spirits-mythical-yokai-%E5%A6%96%E6%80%AA-at-osu-libraries

Japanese mythology: Discovering similarities with other world cultures. (2023, June 1). RoYuMi - Vive Japón. https://royumi.com/en/blogs/blog-de-japon/mitologia-japonesa-descubriendo-similitudes-con-otras-culturas-del-mundo

Japanese raccoon dog. (n.d.). Ultimate Pop Culture Wiki. https://ultimatepopculture.fandom.com/wiki/Japanese_raccoon_dog#In_popular_culture

Japanese religion and spirituality. (2019). Ushistory.org. https://www.ushistory.org/civ/10a.asp

Jimmu. (n.d.). New World Encyclopedia. https://www.newworldencyclopedia.org/entry/Jimmu

Johnson, L. L. (n.d.). *Jingu (c. 201–269).* Encyclopedia. https://www.encyclopedia.com/women/encyclopedias-almanacs-transcripts-and-maps/jingu-c-201-269

Jorōgumo. (n.d.). Yokai. https://yokai.com/jorougumo

Jorogumo: Japanese spider demon. (2022). Kimurakami. https://kimurakami.com/blogs/japan-blog/jorogumo

JTAST. (2016, May 25). *What are "kami?"* Sanpai Japan. https://sanpai-japan.com/2016/05/25/what-are-kami

Kahan, K. (2022). *Japanese Oni: The mysterious world of Japan's historical devils & demons.* Sakuraco. https://sakura.co/blog/japanese-oni-the-mysterious-world-of-japans-historical-devils-demons

Kami. (2009, September 4). BBC. https://www.bbc.co.uk/religion/religions/shinto/beliefs/kami_1.shtml

Kami. (2019). In *Encyclopædia Britannica.* https://www.britannica.com/topic/kami

Kappa. (n.d.). Tokyo Smart. https://www.tokyo-smart.com/en/blog/news/kappa

Kershaw, D. (2022, July 14). *Key characteristics of Japanese mythology.* History Cooperative. https://historycooperative.org/japanese-mythology

Kuchisake onna. (n.d.). Yokai. https://yokai.com/kuchisakeonna

The legendary Empress Jingū. (2015, December 3). KCP International. https://www. kcpinternational.com/2015/12/the-legendary-empress-jingu

Le, L. (2022). *Tanuki magic: Exploring Japan's raccoon dog folklore!* Sakuraco | Japanese Snacks & Candy Subscription Box. https://sakura.co/blog/tanuki-magic-exploring-japans-raccoon-dog-folklore

Littleton, C. S. (1995). Yamatotakeru: An "Arthurian" hero in Japanese tradition. *Asian Folklore Studies, 54*(2), 259–274. JSTOR. https://doi.org/10.2307/1178944

Lloyd, G. (2020). *"Zashiki warashi"—the mythical children who look after your house.* Japan Today. https://japantoday.com/category/features/lifestyle/'zashiki-warashi'-the-mythical-children-who-look-after-your-house

Lopez, K. (2022, November 29). *10 best anime inspired by Japanese mythology.* CBR. https://www.cbr.com/anime-based-on-japanese-mythology/#yuyu-hakusho-features-buddhist-reincarnation

Luscombe, G. (2020). *The first emperor of Japan.* JapanTravel. https://en.japantravel.com/nara/the-first-emperor-of-japan/60970

MacKenzie, D. A. (2014). *Myths of China and Japan.* Literary Licensing, LLC.

Magan, P. (2021, May 20). *Here's how Hinduism and the Japanese religion of Shintoism are very similar.* ED Times. https://edtimes.in/heres-how-hinduism-and-the-japanese-religion-of-shintoism-are-very-similar/

Maguire, S. L. (2011, April 28). *The story of Izanagi and Izanami: A Japanese Creation Myth.* Owlcation; Owlcation. https://owlcation.com/social-sciences/IzanagiandIzunami

Mandal, D. (2023, June 16). *12 major Japanese gods and goddesses you should know about.* Realm of History. https://www.realmofhistory.com/2023/06/16/major-japanese-gods-and-goddesses

Manning, J. (2021, May 19). *Orpheus and Izanagi: How Japan and Greece overlap in love and death.* Academus Education. https://www.academuseducation.co.uk/post/orpheus-and-izanagi-how-japan-and-greece-overlap-in-love-and-death

Martin, R. (2023). *Kitsune.* Encyclopedia Britannica. https://www.britannica.com/topic/Kitsune

Masanobu, K. (2022, July 7). *"Kappa": The terror of Japan's rivers.* Nippon.com. https://www.nippon.com/en/japan-topics/b02505

Masanobu, K. (2022, December 2). *"Tengu": The birdlike demons that became almost divine.* Nippon.com. https://www.nippon.com/en/japan-topics/b02507

Matier, D. (2023). *Japanese folktale: The tale of Momotaro.* LetterPile. https://letter pile.com/creative-writing/Japanese-Folktale-The-Tale-of-Momotaro

McAlpine, H., McAlpine, W., & Kiddell-Monroe, J. (1989). *Japanese tales and legends.* Oxford University Press.

McClain, J. L. (2002). *Japan: A modern history.* Norton.

Mohsin, M. (2020, April 30). *Legend of Kuchisake-onna*. The Business Standard. https://www.tbsnews.net/splash/legend-kuchisake-onna-75496

Morishita, Y. (2020, September 24). *Korean and Japanese Culture—everything you NEED to know*. The Japanese Way. https://thejapaneseway.com/are-korean-and-japanese-culture-similar

Musubi. (n.d.). Encyclopedia Britannica. https://www.britannica.com/topic/musubi

Musubi. (n.d.). Encyclopedia. https://www.encyclopedia.com/religion/dictionaries-thesauruses-pictures-and-press-releases/musubi

Naoki, M. (2019, October 23). *Amaterasu: The Japanese sun goddess*. Nippon. https://www.nippon.com/en/japan-topics/g00748/amaterasu-the-japanese-sun-goddess.html

Ohnuki-Tierney, E. (2002). *Kamikaze, cherry blossoms, and nationalisms: The militarization of aesthetics in Japanese history*. University Of Chicago Press.

Opler, M. E., & Hashima, R. S. (1946). The rice goddess and the fox in Japanese religion and folk practice. *American Anthropologist, 48*(1), 43–53. https://doi.org/10.1525/aa.1946.48.1.02a00050

Ozaki, Y. T. (1908). *The story of Urashima Taro, the fisher lad*. Etc.usf.edu. https://etc.usf.edu/lit2go/72/japanese-fairy-tales/4881/the-story-of-urashima-taro-the-fisher-lad/

Perkins, M. (2019, April 4). *10 of the most important Shinto shrines*. Learn Religions. https://www.learnreligions.com/important-shinto-shrines-4583983

Perkins, M. (2019, April 23). *What are the traditions and practices of Shinto worship?* Learn Religions. https://www.learnreligions.com/shinto-worship-traditions-practices-4570821

Reider, N. T. (2010). *Japanese demon lore: Oni, from ancient times to the present*. Utah State University Press.

Rod, L. (n.d.). *Yamato Takeru*. Rod Shinto. https://www.rodsshinto.com/yamato-takeru

Saaler, S. (2016). *Nationalism and history in contemporary Japan*. The Asia-Pacific Journal. https://apjjf.org/2016/20/Saaler.html

Santos, N. (2019, January 11). *Takamagahara—the High Heaven Plain*. Suki Desu. https://skdesu.com/en/takamagahara-the-plain-of-the-high-sky

Santos, N. (2019, January 6). *Yomi—the world of the dead*. Suki Desu. https://skdesu.com/en/yomi-the-world-of-the-dead

Seybolt, P. J. (n.d.). *China, Korea and Japan: Forgiveness and mourning*. Asia Society. https://asiasociety.org/china-korea-and-japan-forgiveness-and-mourning

Shinto. (2018, April 16). Japan-Guide.com. https://www.japan-guide.com/e/e2056.html

Shinto rituals. (2010). World-Religions-Professor. https://www.world-religions-professor.com/shintorituals.html

Similarities between Indian / Hindu mythology and Japanese mythology. (2022, March 21). GoBookMart. https://gobookmart.com/similarities-between-indian-mythology-or-hindu-mythology-and-japanese-mythology

Similarities between Ireland and Japan (and their folklore). (2020, June 7). Bukimi. https://inkimood.wordpress.com/2020/06/07/similarities-between-ireland-and-japan-and-their-folklore

Similarities to other mythology. (n.d.). Shimane. https://www.kankou-shimane.com/en/japanesemythology/kojiki/4.html

Smith, M. (2019, August 29). *Japanese mythology: Cosmogony.* Canadianstudies.isp.msu.edu. https://canadianstudies.isp.msu.edu/news_article/22292

Smits, G. (2006). Shaking up Japan: Edo society and the 1855 catfish picture prints. *Journal of Social History, 39*(4), 1045–1078. https://doi.org/10.1353/jsh.2006.0057

Star, M. (2020, June 22). *The Japanese creation myth.* JAPAN THIS! https://japanthis.com/2020/06/22/the-japanese-creation-myth

The story of Momotarō. (2012, December 4). KCP International. https://www.kcpinternational.com/2012/12/momotaro

Takeuchi, L. (n.d.). *Yamamba.* Byu Bakemono. https://bakemono.lib.byu.edu/yokai/yamamba

The tale of Urashima Taro. (2014). Public Relations Office. https://www.gov-online.go.jp/eng/publicity/book/hlj/html/201407/201407_09_en.html

Tanaka, S., Brownlee, J. S., & Mehl, M. (1998). Japanese historians and the national myths, 1600-1945: the age of the gods and Emperor Jinmu. *Choice Reviews Online, 36*(01), 36-0482. https://doi.org/10.5860/choice.36-0482

Tengu. (n.d.). New World Encyclopedia. https://www.newworldencyclopedia.org/entry/tengu

Tengu no Kakuremino—folk legends. (n.d.). Kids Web Japan. https://web-japan.org/kidsweb/folk/tengu/tengu01.html

Top 10 traditional Japanese festivals. (2020, January 23). Japan Wireless. https://jw-webmagazine.com/japanese-festivals

The trickster animal spirit: Tanuki. (n.d.). Japan House. https://japanhouse.illinois.edu/education/insights/tanuki

Tsuchigumo. (n.d.). Byu Bakemono. https://bakemono.lib.byu.edu/yokai/tsuchigumo

Tsuchigumo. (n.d.). Japan Box. https://thejapanbox.com/blogs/japanese-mythology/tsuchigumo

Urashima Taro. (2024). Kyuhoshi. https://www.kyuhoshi.com/urashima-taro

What is Kitsune? Types, tales & everything you need to know. (n.d.). Japanese Oni Masks. https://japaneseonimasks.com/blogs/magazine/what-is-kitsune

What is Jorōgumo? Yōkai in Japanese folklore. (2022). Mythology Planet. https://mythologyplanet.com/jorogumo-yokai-japanese-folklore

What Is Oni? The mythology of the Japanese Oni in folklore. (n.d.). Japanese Oni Masks. https://japaneseonimasks.com/blogs/magazine/what-is-oni

What is the Matsuri (Japanese cultural festival)? (2018). ANA. https://www.ana.co.jp/en/ph/japan-travel-planner/japanese-festival-omatsuri/0000001.html

What is Tsuchigumo? Yōkai in Japanese mythology. (2022, December 31). Mythology Planet. https://mythologyplanet.com/tsuchigumo-yokai-japanese-mythology

What is Yomi in Japanese mythology: Unveiling the secrets of the underworld. (2023, October 21). Old World Gods. https://oldworldgods.com/japanese/what-is-yomi-in-japanese-mythology

Williams, J. (n.d.). *The Cinderella tales of Niigata.* Keiwa. https://www.keiwa-c.ac.jp/wp-content/uploads/2012/12/kiyo13-13.pdf

Wood, M. (2019). *In search of myths & heroes. What is a myth?* Pbs.org. https://www.pbs.org/mythsandheroes/myths_what.html

Wright, G. (2022, November 29). *Amaterasu.* Mythopedia. https://mythopedia.com/topics/amaterasu

Wright, G. (2022, November 29). *Susanoo.* Mythopedia. https://mythopedia.com/topics/susanoo

Wright, G. (2022, November 29). *Tsukuyomi.* Mythopedia. https://mythopedia.com/topics/tsukuyomi

Xavier, C. (2020, April 24). *Japanese gods and mythology: The Shinto religion.* History Cooperative. https://historycooperative.org/japanese-gods-and-the-shinto-religion

Yamato Takeru. (n.d.). Myth and Folklore Wiki. https://mythus.fandom.com/wiki/Yamato_Takeru

Yamauba. (n.d.). Yokai. https://yokai.com/yamauba

Yong, C. (2023). *118 Shinto gods and goddesses to know about.* Owlcation—Education. https://owlcation.com/humanities/shinto-gods-goddesses-kojiki-nihon-shoki

Yu, A. C. (2024). *Musuhi (life-producing spirits).* Japanese Wiki. https://www.japanesewiki.com/Shinto/Musuhi%20(Life-producing%20spirits).html

Yu, A. C. (2023). *Takamanohara (Plain of High Heaven).* Japanese Wiki. https://www.japanesewiki.com/literature/Takamanohara%20(plain%20of%20high%20heaven).html

Yu, A. C. (n.d.). *Tanokami.* Japanese Wiki. https://www.japanesewiki.com/Shinto/Tanokami.html

Yu, A. C. (2024). *Yashiki-gami (Household God).* Japanese Wiki. https://www.japanesewiki.com/shrines/Yashiki-gami%20(Household%20God).html

Zashiki-warashi. (n.d.). TV Tropes. https://tvtropes.org/pmwiki/pmwiki.php/Main/ZashikiWarashi

Zashiki warashi. (n.d.). Yokai.com. https://yokai.com/zashikiwarashi

Printed in Great Britain
by Amazon

55150559R00079